Birds In Your Garden

A month-by-month guide

Birds In Your Garden

A month-by-month guide

Tony Soper
and Roger Lovegrove

Grange
BOOKS

Published by Grange Books
An imprint of Grange Books Limited
The Grange
Grange Yard
London SE1 3AG

ISBN 1 85627 351 2

Reprinted 1993

First published by Webb & Bower
(Publishers) Limited 1989

Text Copyright © 1989 Tony Soper/Roger Lovegrove
Illustrations Copyright © 1989 Webb & Bower/John Busby

Printed and bound in Singapore.

CONTENTS

Introduction

There is probably no other nation in the world which holds the domestic garden in such possessive affection and esteem as the British. If the Englishman's home is his castle, his garden is the island on which it sits. Of the fourteen million to fifteen million homes in Britain probably ten million or so have a garden of one sort or another. These gardens may vary from the narrowest interpretation of a backyard with a window-box, to the estate agent's euphemistic 'quarter acre', the generosity of Buckingham Palace or the magnificence of Bodnant or Powis Castle.

Nonetheless, however possessive the gardener may be or however manicured and controlled his oasis may appear he can never claim exclusiveness. He shares his patch with an immense, albeit unseen, community of wildlife: an inter-acting multitude of tiny insects and invertebrates, microscopic plants as well as more familiar ones, animals and birds. Be the garden however humble, these industrious, interwoven kingdoms are the forces which give the garden its life. They nourish, fertilize, aerate, decay and recycle, sustain and renew. They feed on and from each other and occasionally they manifest themselves as nuisances on the plants we ourselves try to grow. Do not wage chemical war or attempt to fight against these life giving forces. Control the unwanted excesses of weeds when necessary; discourage undesirable species – rats, couch grass or slugs – but always recognise the fact that the whole garden is a living entity. Consider too the benefits of the increasing trend towards organic rather than chemical gardening.

A garden is more than a recreation area, a place of beauty or a vegetable patch. It is an opportunity to achieve around our home a private island of even greater attraction and richness. Whatever the primary aim there is always the scope to make it even more attractive for wild birds and thereby a more exciting and rewarding place as well. This book sets out to help you to achieve this by describing and suggesting a variety of the steps you can take month by month throughout the year to attract birds into your garden.

It is calculated that there are already several million bird watchers in Britain (there are half a million members of the Royal Society for the Protection of Birds alone) and the great majority of these are people who simply take pleasure from watching birds in the garden through the windows of their homes. A simple understanding of the needs of different birds and how to provide these can quickly result in increasing both the numbers and variety of birds which will use the garden. At a time when open countryside is still being devoured in Britain at the rate of about 40,000 acres each year, the role of gardens in sustaining our native wildlife becomes more important all the time; already these gardens total almost three quarters of a million acres. Let this book help you make your garden a better place for birds and other wildlife – and thus for you!

JANUARY

A pale January sun only thinly disguises the reality of deepest winter at a time when sheer survival is the consuming aim for garden birds. Literally millions of small woodland, farm and forest birds from north and central Europe have come to the relative mildness of Britain to escape the frozen grip of a Continental winter and join our resident birds in the daily challenge for survival. Even in a comparatively mild British winter times will be hard: insect food is difficult to come by, earthworms and other soil invertebrates are deep down and mostly out of reach, the autumn bonanza of fruits and berries has been imprudently stripped and wastefully exploited in the shortening days of late autumn and early winter. Each week, each day this huge number of birds will forage and compete for the ever-diminishing stock of wild foods. Many will perish in the course of the winter, while others – the strongest and most successful – will survive to breed the next generation. The recent (1986) *Atlas of Wintering Birds in Britain and Ireland* produced by the British Trust for Ornithology (BTO) and the Irish Wildbird Conservancy attempts to put estimates on Britain's mid-winter bird populations. From this it can be calculated that by the turn of the year the British countryside and towns, parks and gardens support between them something like 240 million 'garden' birds! It would be a rash person who dared to estimate what proportion of such a total is dependent on gardens as opposed to the open countryside; obviously the proportion varies greatly from one species to another and also from winter to winter, and area to area. Could we dare to speculate that perhaps as many as a quarter of these birds use gardens at some stage of the winter? This would be perhaps sixty million birds. After all eighty per cent of our homes have a garden of some sort making a total of some ten million gardens with an overall area of about 700,000 acres; but of course the majority of garden birds live in more than one garden at a time. What is certain is that we have an immense capacity to influence the survival and welfare of these birds. Our gardens are an immense resource for wildlife at a time when other good habitats in the countryside are shrinking at an alarming rate, and one of their important features is the enormous variety which individual gardens present. It is not simply as a source of artificial food that they are used, but also as places of shelter providing a range of safe sites for nesting and roosting. Our gardens are indeed one of the richest bird habitats in the country.

The colourful waxwing is a rare winter visitor to berry crops in a few privileged gardens in some years.

Table 1

Estimated numbers of some familiar garden birds in the British Isles, mid-winter. (Figures taken from BTO *Atlas of Wintering Birds in Britain and Ireland.*)

Wren	*12–20 million*	*Blue tit*	*15 million*
Dunnock	*20 ,,*	*Great tit*	*10 ,,*
Robin	*10 ,,*	*Nuthatch*	*60,000 +*
Blackbird	*14–20 ,,*	*Magpie*	*750,000 +*
Song thrush	*6–10 ,,*	*Starling*	*37 million*
Redwing	*1 + ,,*	*House sparrow*	*10–15 ,,*
Goldcrest	*2–4 ,,*	*Chaffinch*	*30 ,,*
Blackcap	*3000*	*Bullfinch*	*1 ,,*

What is a garden bird?

The great majority of birds which regularly use our gardens belong to the order of passerines, or perching birds. This is by far the largest, most complex and highly developed order and it embraces all Britain's familiar families of song birds — thrushes, finches, starling, warblers, wren, etc — as well as swallows and martins, crows, cuckoo, tits, nuthatch, treecreeper, pipits and wagtails. In evolutionary terms these families are the most advanced of bird species and many of them, as we can readily see, have adapted beneficially to living cheek by jowl with man, to the extent of quite heavy dependence in some cases, eg house sparrow, house martin, starling. It is, therefore, the birds from this huge order that we are most able to influence and cater for in our gardens, first and foremost by the provision of food in the harsh days of winter.

The passerines however do not have exclusive rights to the surroundings of our homes. Gardens are as varied as we choose to make them and no two are the same. Depending on the size, position and character of a garden, a few species from other orders of birds will occur. Occasional gardens may have kingfishers, many will have pigeons or doves, some will attract herons to pilfer from the fish pond, or sparrowhawks which profit from the abundance of small birds attracted there; in others there are tawny owls, moorhens on the pond edge and a woodpecker foraging in the nearby woodlands. There are ways in which we can provide for almost all these species, and one of the rewards of bird gardening, and especially winter feeding, is the certainty that the unexpected will turn up from time to time, be it a colourful waxwing, a rare and tiny firecrest or a wandering family of partridges.

Mid-winter — a time of passing

It almost goes without saying that winter is the season when most birds die. The winter mortality of some of those birds which remain with us all year can be enormous in a really prolonged and severe winter. Small insectivorous birds are at greatest risk, such as wren, goldcrest and long-tailed tit. They are such tiny birds that they have very little potential for storing body fat and are therefore particularly susceptible to extremes of cold and shortage of food. For example, the wren population may number well in excess of five million pairs in peak years but this number will be reduced to no more than a tenth of this by a really cold winter, and will take two or three years to build up to a peak again.

Death is the ultimate price a bird pays for inefficiency or inexperience in winter. It is all quite predictable. Most of Britain's winter passerines have produced relatively large broods of young — some of them successive broods — and a high proportion will have died by the end of their first winter. Inexperience is the real killer. Once a bird has lived long enough to breed for the first time its chances of survival to relative old age are good. By this time it has endured at least one winter, avoided predation by sparrowhawk, tawny owl or cat and, if it is migratory (perhaps from Scandinavia or central Europe) it has proved its ability to withstand long overland or overseas flights. So the young and the unwitting are the individuals which will succumb first to the rigours and perils of winter. Throughout this season, however, many thousands of these winter song birds, adults and young alike, are kept alive by the extra food which is offered by householders. There is no doubting the effect which artificial feeding can have on these

Dead goldcrest: this is a time of high mortality for many of our resident birds.

populations: garden bird feeding will enable many thousands to survive which would otherwise fail to live through the winter.

Table 1 on the previous page shows the estimated numbers of some of our most familiar garden birds at the onset of winter. As winter progresses the numbers will reduce steadily. To take dunnock as an example, it is estimated that there may be some five million breeding pairs in the British Isles (ie ten million breeding individuals). It is an extremely sedentary species and very few Continental immigrants arrive to swell the winter numbers which are thought to be in the order of twenty million in December as the result of the output of the breeding season. Over the following fourteen or sixteen weeks of winter and early spring the dunnock population will crash to about half this total thus taking it back again to the breeding level. By March some thirty-five per cent of the adult birds have succumbed (about three and a half million) as well as seven to eight million juvenile birds! How many of us have willingly put in time and effort to restore a sick or injured dunnock or other small bird in winter?

Blue tit merry-go-round

In winter, the first two hours of daylight are a period of intense feeding. Eight short, cold hours of daylight and sixteen hours of deep cold and darkness mean that the early morning feeding is crucial to build up the body's reserves again after the energy loss required to maintain body heat during the long night. In these early hours of the morning the bird-table traffic is fast and furious. From the inside warmth of the window we can puzzle and wonder just how many different individuals take advantage of the feast provided. The blue tits keep coming and going — there must surely be at least twenty different ones. Not so many great tits . . . perhaps six or eight. Clouds of starlings plundering the food as though they have only five minutes to live and their lives depend on it, and a score or more of house sparrows. A nuthatch which makes planned, deliberate and exclusive visits to the peanut feeder; two birds actually, because we can tell the male from the female. A dunnock gleans tiny morsels fallen from the table or left by the ravening hordes of starlings; but is it the same one which slides quietly out of the garden border each time? A handful of chaffinches, two or three bullish robins . . . and so on.

Try to work out for yourself how many individuals may be involved at your bird table. In many cases it will be impossible but there are a few useful clues and some of the birds will fairly readily be identifiable as individuals. Some will have their own idiosyncrasies; always feed at the same spot or in the same manner, or will invariably approach from a particular direction. Others will have minor differences of plumage; a broken feather, a dark smudge or similar distinguishing mark. Look carefully at these daily visitors to the bird table and it will be surprising how many you can begin to recognise. It is fun to try to work out just how many birds are benefitting from the food you provide. The real truth of these numbers will elude you but most of us would be truly surprised at the actual numbers involved if we did but know them. It is a safe bet that our estimate of 'at least twenty blue tits' is far removed from actuality. Mixed winter parties of tits will usually comprise a majority of blue tits and great tits but will also be accompanied by a few long-tailed tits, nuthatches, goldcrests, treecreepers and the odd willow tit or even a lesser spotted woodpecker. They will forage together daily through hedgerow, woodland and garden. This daily round is not an aimless, opportunistic or hit-and-miss wandering but carefully follows a deliberate route based on acquired knowledge and an experienced familiarity with the best feeding areas; it may well be varied from day to day to take account of weather conditions. As the blue tit bandwagon rolls round each day it will pick up and drop off other passengers *en route*; willow tits and marsh tits remain paired and on territory through the winter, for example, and as the merry-go-round passes through they may well join it and then leave again once it passes on out of their territory. Your bird table is most certainly *en route* too, probably as the major station for most of these travellers. The shy ones and the insectivores – long-tailed tits, treecreepers, goldcrests – will stay in the background and appear less willingly at the table, even though birds as small as this must spend ninety to ninety-five per cent of daylight time feeding. So keep the table fully charged! Don't feel that by 11.30 am 'the greedy blue tits have had enough for today' because you may have fed the 8.30, the 9.45 and the 10.40 arrivals, but there are still a few more bandwagons to pass by yet!

The number of blue tits and others calling in the course of a day is therefore likely to be far in excess of your guess. In a small isolated garden (30 yd × 15 yd) at Criccieth in Gwynedd more than 100 different individual blue tits were found to be visiting the bird table daily in mid-winter. In suburban gardens at least 200 blue tits daily may use favoured bird tables, but the turnover throughout the course of a winter will be far in excess of this. In a Buckinghamshire garden on the outskirts of High Wycombe a 'small party' of greenfinches came regularly for wheat put down in January and February. When the greenfinches were caught for ringing purposes, 120 different birds were handled the first day!

The unassuming dunnock lives the great part of its life at ground level; a shuffling and undistinguished bird, it has a complex and interesting life style.

The bold markings on the male great tit (left) are in contrast to the less strongly patterned female.

Ivy – a January plant

Ivy is one of the very best plants to grow in the bird garden. It offers several major benefits for birds and a number of genuine uses for the gardener; moreover there is no truth in the old story that ivy kills the trees on which it grows, except possibly in very rare cases when it may smother the growing crown. It is often a maligned and ill-treated plant, but is in fact one of the bird gardener's most valuable natural assets. Use ivy as a wall climber on outhouses or sheds, or to straggle over tree stumps and fences, as well as encouraging it as a tree climber. Because it is evergreen and produces a dense foliage it is an important plant for winter roosting: wrens love it and thrushes, house sparrows and dunnocks too are secure from

predators in the secret depths of its thick leaves. It will only flower when in good light but its peculiarly late flowering season in September–October means that the berry crop develops in late winter at the time when most other wild berries have been used up. By January the clusters of black fruits start to become available to birds and are great favourites of woodpigeon, mistle thrush, blackbird, song thrush, some of the redwings and overwintering blackcaps.

Ivy is a native plant, very attractive to insects, especially in the flowering season, but also at other times of year too. This means that it provides especially good foraging for birds such as the wren, which can explore the innumerable shady recesses for spiders, woodlice or earwigs. In autumn and early spring willow warblers and chiff chaffs feed amongst its leaves and it is always a happy hunting ground for tits, never more so than in the difficult days of winter.

In the breeding season its dense cover again makes it attractive as a nest site for a wide range of garden birds. Wrens use it regularly; blackbirds and song thrushes too can use it early in the season before other bushes have leaf cover. Dunnocks, chaffinches, greenfinches, linnets and spot-

A roving winter flock of tits, treecreepers and others.

ted flycatchers often conceal their nests in its canopy. Woodpigeons, turtle doves and collared doves frequently build among the upper levels.

No, ivy is not a plant to malign. It will grow on almost any soil however poor, and contrary to another myth, does not suck the goodness out of its host trees which it uses solely for climbing support, grasping tightly with the root-like hairs on its stems. The common ivy (*Hedera helix*) has dark green glossy leaves, but several other variegated ivies are readily obtainable nowadays and will add year round colour while still providing all the benefits of the familiar wild form for birds and a host of other garden wildlife.

A garden master plan

January provides little opportunity to get out into the garden to do any of the inevitable jobs which always await. Either the ground is too wet to work or it is frozen solid. You replenish the food supplies on the bird table daily and vital drinking water is kept ice free, but otherwise this is the time for watching from indoors and pondering all the things that should have been done last year and weren't. We cannot let them go another year. This is the time for the 'master plan'!

Perhaps the greatest thing about bird gardening is that it is virtually guaranteed to succeed. The

Ivy is one of the most important wildlife plants.

The great spotted woodpecker is one of the most colourful birds which may be attracted regularly to gardens.

degree to which it succeeds will be unpredictable but it is doubtful if there is any garden in the country, however small or large, however bleakly exposed or metropolitan which cannot be made more attractive to birds. Provide appropriate food for birds in winter and they will find it; provide safe roosting sites and nest sites and the offer is unlikely to be refused. Even in the meanest city back-yard garden house sparrows, starlings and feral pigeons will be attracted to food; put up an RSPB tit feeder full of peanuts, or a hanging scrap basket and the urban blue tit, grimy and smoke-dulled but every bit as resourceful as its brighter country cousin, will find it before long, and where one leads others are sure to follow. No garden anywhere is too mean to be unresponsive to a sensible plan to improve it for birds.

Now, in the depths of winter and confined indoors, is the time to consider carefully the various things that we can do month by month through the year to make the garden a more attractive place for birds. The justification for us doing this is simple: birds living in our gardens and around our houses bring us endless pleasure, interest, excitement and sometimes amusement. In return we can provide positively for them in a variety of ways to make their lives easier and safer. Through the application of a little knowledge and skill we can also increase the number and variety of birds which choose to share our garden with us.

It is well to remember that a bird has relatively few basic requirements but that several of them lend themselves to our help; in this respect, if we keep our sights clear, there is at least simplicity on our side. Any part of our garden plan must necessarily apply to one or more of these basic requirements.

Food – wild foods which birds will garner direct from the plants and soil in the garden, but also food specially provided in winter.

Nest sites – both 'naturally' provided in bushes, shrubs and banks and artificially supplied through nest boxes etc.

Shelter and roost sites

Water – for drinking and bathing.

Protection from predators

In starting to formulate the outlines of any plan to suit an individual garden we must bear these requirements in mind all the time. Do not forget however that it is *your* garden and it must also fulfil your needs either for garden produce, to look colourful and pleasing to the eye, or simply for the children or dog to play in.

Use your plan to try to bring as much variety to the garden as you are able. The reward for diversity will be that you attract a wide range of birds. For a start aim to produce different tiers of ground and vegetation, thinking of all the variations from the flat lawn to banks, rockery, the boundary hedges, walls or fences, shrubbery, trees and finally the house itself. If there is not already natural water available in the garden, plan to make a pond, however modest, or at least introduce some form of drinking and bathing facility. Are you providing enough evergreen cover and is it of the right native species? This will not only help produce a sheltered garden but can also contribute to the food supply for birds and other wildlife.

You will want to consider what the scope is for trees in the garden. Perhaps you are lucky in having a woodland edge in any case or you may benefit from trees on your neighbour's boundary, in which case you may be able to 'borrow' the benefits without having to plant further ones yourself. The chances are however that you will have some scope for additional trees of some description. You will then wish to select carefully to ensure that you are choosing ones that will still fit into the garden when they are full grown in forty or fifty years time or more, and will be of maximum benefit to birds both now and in the future. You will almost certainly be choosing native trees but it is a long-term investment and you can't afford to get it wrong.

A decent sized lawn is almost a prerequisite in your bird garden. If it is well kept and regularly mown it will provide an important open feeding area for blackbird, song thrush, robin, starling and pied wagtail. It will also provide you with the best opportunity to see the birds in the open. In the garden beds around the lawn you have to consider the advantages of growing selected plants which are attractive to insects (and thus to birds). Many familiar flowers are ones which will bring instant colour to the garden but their return in terms of benefits to garden wildlife, in the form of insects or seeds which can be eaten by birds, may be poor.

The development of shrubbery, either free-standing or against walls and fences is another important area of decision. Not only will it play an important part in contributing to the whole pattern of shelter and nest sites, as well as the seasonal colours in the garden, but it will have a key role in the provision of berries for winter food if the selection is right.

At this time of strategic planning the main question surrounding the provision of winter food may simply be whether you have the right area in which to do it. Does it offer enough scope? Are the feeding birds being tempted too close to cover where potential four-legged predators can lie in wait? Can you see the feeding area satisfactorily from the house windows? If you do not have the right answers to these questions it may well be that the garden has to have some basic alterations this year.

Finally it must be borne in mind that the neatest and tidiest gardens will not be the best for birds. Try hard to build in some areas or corners of rough ground where nettles, thistles, knapweed, rank grasses, docks and other rough vegetation can flourish. Whether or not it offends the tidy gardener's eye, the birds will love it.

Unless you are particularly fortunate it is unlikely that your garden can adopt all the principles suggested here. Select those which are most appropriate to your own garden and your own needs. Throughout the other sections of this book we shall look in more detail at each of the subjects outlined. For now, make this the New Year bird garden resolution — the Plan For Action!

An all-the-year hedge

Perhaps your boundary hedges and fences are already determined for you but if not, what a wonderful chance you have to establish your own architect-designed home-built bird hedge. The bird garden needs good thick thorny hedges, evergreen at least in part, nice and tall but with plenty of bottom and producing as many berries as possible. It must be high enough and thick enough to produce genuine shelter from strong cold winds and should be of native shrubs. Ideally

it will contain a mixture of the most familiar hedgerow species — hawthorn, blackthorn, holly and hazel and perhaps berberis (a non-native) and privet. Several of these species have the advantage of being thorny and therefore fairly cat proof, and holly, privet and (some) berberis have the further advantage of being evergreen. If your hedge is sufficiently long it will pay you to encourage one or two selected shoots to grow through as standard trees, possibly hawthorn, holly or hazel. Trim the side shoots immediately above hedge height and these trees will reward you with more winter berries and nuts than several yards of hedgerow.

The native privet (*Lingustrum vulgare*) is a commendable hedgerow shrub producing a good harvest of berries (bullfinches are very fond of them) if not clipped too hard in summer and autumn. Note however that the popular golden privet, although attractive to look at, does not produce berries or thorns and is a very poor alternative. There are many berberis varieties, some with red berries, some with black and a selection is listed on page 113. For further advice put yourself in the hands of your nurseryman to select one which is evergreen and prolific. Yew is also a good evergreen hedge plant with dense cover but is slow growing and extremely toxic for ponies and farm animals should they be able to reach it and graze. In addition it does not bear berries if clipped regularly. Although they are deciduous, beech and hornbeam retain their dead leaves through the winter and thus give good shelter and a very sturdy hedge.

Hedges are of major importance to birds all

The hedge bottom is the most important bird-foraging area in any garden.

16

year round. Apart from the fruit which they bear themselves, they provide rich opportunities for birds to forage for small insects among their twigs, leaves and buds. The hedge bottom is probably the most important foraging place in the garden for ground feeding birds in winter. Blackbirds regularly search among the leaf litter there as do song thrushes, dunnocks, robins and great tits. The hedge bottom is a rich hunting area for small mammals as well as birds and it very rarely gets completely covered when the rest of the garden may be snowbound.

Do not trim the hedge in autumn more than is necessary for good husbandry or tidiness. If appropriate let it mature to six feet or so and it will give the garden privacy and allow the birds freedom from constant disturbance from the roadside or the neighbours. If it is good and thorny it will do a lot to keep the cats at bay!

Woodpeckers and suet sticks

Great spotted woodpeckers are strongly territorial birds throughout the year and therefore they are only likely to visit the garden regularly where it lies close to the general boundaries of their territory. In winter they show a slight tendency to wander and are becoming more common as visitors to garden feeding stations. At this season their feeding becomes a little more catholic and includes tree seeds – beech mast, acorns, hazel nuts, hornbeam and some conifer seeds – as well as invertebrates excavated from decaying timber. This latter habit provides the clue for a simple way to tempt great spotted woodpeckers to become regular winter visitors, because they have a partiality for suet (or dripping) which, once discovered, becomes irresistible to them. Take a short length of log, birch is ideal because it is soft and woodpeckers associate well with it, and drill a series of holes in it 1 in (2.5 cm) deep which you then pack with suet. Tits and nuthatches will use it as well but the woodpeckers will give you hours of entertainment. They are, after all, one of the most colourful birds to attract to the garden although you should remember that they are very timid and may be reluctant to come if the feeder is too close to the house; the farther away the more likely they are to use it.

A variation of the suet stick can be developed through the use of a larger log or post 'planted' in a selected spot or by taking advantage of an existing tree stump which may make a welcome feature. Great spotted woodpeckers will also visit the bird table and are as adept as titmice at feeding from hanging peanut feeders or scrap baskets. Also, if you are amongst those whose surplus of Christmas nuts usually lingers until the following year, crack the nuts open, take some out and wedge the kernels firmly into posts and crevices where the woodpeckers and nuthatches will enjoy chiseling at them.

Winter warblers

Within the past twenty years the blackcap has increased considerably as a wintering bird in southern Britain. At a time when all other migrant warblers are deep in the heat of West or Central Africa, these blackcaps have evolved a strategy that allows them to winter with us and avoid making the long journey west of the Sahara. In fact these birds are already travellers as most of them are not left-overs from our summer breeders, but migrants from breeding populations in eastern or northern Europe which arrive here in autumn. They are commonest in suburban gardens and appear to prefer soft berries so long as supplies last, after which they become more omnivorous and will feed on a wide variety of bird table foods. It is likely that their willingness to join the bird table community is a key to their unquestioned ability to survive even some of Britain's coldest winters.

The chiff chaff is an even more frail and improbable wintering warbler, but for a long time small numbers have remained through the winter as residents. Most are found in the southern counties of England, Wales and Ireland but unlike the blackcaps they remain insectivorous and suffer heavy casualties in severe winters. They are not drawn to garden feeding stations and are mostly to be found in the vicinity of watersides, among willows, alders, reed beds and the like.

Garden birdwatch – the family day

For over a decade the Young Ornithologists' Club (YOC) – the junior branch of the RSPB – has organised an annual Garden Birdwatch. Although it was originally launched as a children's event it has become extremely popular and has become, par excellence, the family garden birdwatching event of the year. It usually takes place on the last weekend of January and from 1988 it took on an international flavour with the involvement of participants in several other European countries.

The basic object of the Garden Birdwatch is to keep a tally of all birds landing in the garden in the course of a one-hour period, mainly by recording the highest numbers of each species which are on the ground or perched nearby at any one time. Many thousands of families often take part and indeed the aim is to involve as many children and adults as possible in a worthwhile project thereby encouraging them to take an interest in the birds in their garden. For many it is their first active participation in anything to do with birds and may well lead to a lifetime's interest. It is a simple and worthwhile project which even the very youngest in the family can take part in and enjoy.

From the thousands of results which are sent in to the YOC, the organisers analyse the findings and discover what the 'top ten' birds were on the weekend in question. Results can be compared from year to year, region to region and contrasts between town and country can be identified. So if you want to join in the annual family bird watching day without having to set foot outside on a cold January day, write to the YOC, The Lodge, Sandy, Beds, SG19 2DL with a stamped, addressed envelope and they will send you the details.

Blackcaps may increasingly be seen in the winter garden. These are mainly birds that have moved west from eastern Europe instead of travelling south to Africa with the main part of the population.

FEBRUARY

The days are just a little longer now and the first tentative signs of plant growth persuade us that half the winter is now behind, even though the bitterest weather could still be ahead. It may seem premature that on a sunny day at this time of year, or in the early mornings, there is a surprising amount of bird song when emerging spring is still several weeks away. Where wildlife is concerned our thinking is often too constrained and unimaginative; it is all too easy to allow ourselves to think of the birds' annual calendar as fitting in conveniently with our own ideas of the beginnings and ends of seasons whereas very often this is far removed from actuality. If there is a true 'end' of the year for garden birds it might best be found in the dog days of summer when the breeding season is finished, young birds are becoming independent, plumage is being renewed and it is a period of relative inactivity. Now, however, in the month of February, there is a lot of activity and although survival dominates all other considerations many garden birds have been making preparations for the next breeding season for some time.

Many of the blue tits in the daily foraging flocks are already paired and the males will sing sporadically if the weather is warm. Adult great tits retain their breeding territories through the year and will advertise them increasingly now as the days slowly lengthen. Marsh tit and willow tit are habitually faithful both to their partners and their breeding areas throughout the remainder of the year. Wrens too are strongly territorial in winter and will sing at any time to advertise and defend their chosen areas as the competition for the best sites probably began as early as last August. By February, given any encouragement by the weather they will make the first moves to establish spring territories and the song will therefore intensify even in the relative depths of winter. The most successful breeders are always the older experienced birds and they will already be competing for the prime territories. In the hills of the north and west the ravens are repairing their nests and in the pine forests it is already the middle of the breeding season for crossbills! These strange birds, which feed on an exclusive diet of seeds dexterously extracted from the pine cones, sometimes breed in autumn but their main season starts in the mid-winter so that they can feed their young at a time when individual cones are beginning to open up and the seed is easier to exploit. Early pairs of blackbirds and song thrushes are thinking of breeding and the mistle thrush, regularly the earliest of all our breeding garden birds, is singing in full voice before February is through.

The male dunnock has a strange single-wing-flicking display in its courtship ritual.

Dynamic dunnock

The dunnock is the archetypal little brown bird, dun-coloured, shy and skulking. In fact if you look more closely it has an attractive delicate grey head and chest, rich rufous back streaked with black and a bright reddish-brown eye. It emerges into the open almost apologetically from the hedge bottom or the garden border to move mouse-like in a sort of legless shuffle on the lawn edge or to pick unobtrusively for morsels on the ground below the bird table. Few of our garden birds spend as much time at ground level as the self-effacing dunnock. It is a successful bird however and in the 'top five' of our most numerous species; few gardens of any size are without their resident dunnocks. At the turn of the year the males are already singing and by February pair formation is under way and song is regular and more intensive. Its matrimonial entanglements are so complicated that it is frequently unrealistic to talk about 'pairs' of dunnocks. To start with several males may well have overlapping territories and therefore it is difficult to decide even how many males there are in the garden. Some mating is in conventional monogamous pairs but other pairings may comprise one male and several females, several males and one female or even communal groupings of several of each sex! Sorting out what is what with the dunnocks in a large garden should keep you engrossed for the season. During courtship the birds have a strange single-wing flicking display and later it may well be the dunnock's nest which will play host to the cuckoo's egg for they are the most important host species for cuckoos among all our garden birds.

Coping with frost and snow

It is not the sheer intensity of winter cold which is the real killer for birds, but the fact that they are denied access to the necessary intake of food when the supplies are frozen in the ground or covered by deep snow. Given that a bird can get all the food it needs in the short days of winter, it can withstand extremely low temperatures, the more so if it has a good roosting place at night where its heat loss can be kept to a minimum. Most of the daylight hours must be devoted to taking in food to build up instant reserves of lipid, a type of 'fast food' body fat which the bird will use to keep warm through the forthcoming night. A bird's problems in this respect are in direct proportion to its body size. The small birds such as wren, goldcrest, long-tailed tit and chiff chaff have relatively big surface areas compared to their tiny bodies and their rate of heat loss is correspondingly high with the result that they have to feed feverishly all through the day in order to store enough lipid to see them through the night. In the course of each day they will need to take in about a third of their body weight of food. The larger birds, whose rates of heat loss are proportionately less in relation to their size, are more likely to achieve their feeding targets in shorter time than their smallest relations. This is one of the reasons why the smaller birds are the first to arrive at the feeding station in the morning and will be the last ones seen there at nightfall as they must spend the maximum possible time feeding. In winter a bird such as a chaffinch or blackbird may consistently be twenty to twenty-five per cent heavier at the time it goes to roost than it is during the summer half of the year; by morning most of this extra will have been used up again.

When either ice or heavy snow covers the ground they bring the most difficult problems for those birds which normally rely on invertebrate food which is in the soil or seeds and other food items which are picked up from the surface: lapwing, black-headed gull, snipe, rook, skylark, and most of the thrushes will be amongst the first to suffer. With the food supplies covered their problem is immediate and they have to bring in alternative strategies quickly. The first option they have is to move out fast and try to go beyond the snow belt. Several of the species mentioned above are renowned for hard weather movements and normally, like the best of our weather forecasters, they will accurately anticipate and move out ahead of it rather than wait until it arrives and then have to respond. Otherwise they are forced to explore more precarious areas of open ground where they are more vulnerable to predators and would not normally expect to go. This may take them to unfrozen wateredges, farmyards and buildings, refuse tips and garden feeding places. It is always in circumstances like these that the completely unexpected bird may arrive in the garden. If both these strategies fail, the birds are in deep trouble and casualties will be high if the frost and snow lasts. It is difficult for the bird gardener to do much about frozen ground and ice, but when heavy snow has fallen every effort should be made to clear some areas (you will hopefully clear the area around the feeding station anyway, otherwise food put down there will quickly be lost in the soft snow). You can also help by clearing areas where birds forage regularly – the hedge bottoms, the edges of the shrubbery, the garden borders

The Garden Bird Survey shows that sparrowhawks are among the top twenty or so of common garden birds.

against the house walls and the base of the compost heap.

It is an ill-wind that blows nobody any good and the severe weather probably does no harm to a bird like the sparrowhawk. This predator needs about 2 oz (50 g) of food per day, equivalent to three sparrow-sized birds or one blackbird, and under the circumstances of hard weather when many of the small birds may have to take unacceptable levels of risk, hunting is pretty easy for the sparrowhawk. Of course, if it kills something as large as a woodpigeon, or one of the fantails off the neighbour's roof, the supply will last more than one day so keep watch because the sparrowhawk will return the next day to reclaim its prey. Don't look harshly on the sparrowhawk because surely he has as much right to the food supply on the bird table as the song birds being fed there daily? It is just that he would rather take his food live and deal with it himself. Remember too the vast surplus of young birds produced each year which have to reduce by one means and another before next breeding season: the European butter mountains and wine lakes have got nothing on the juvenile bird-meat surplus which the sparrowhawk will harvest.

Roosting and insulation

Birds have fairly high body temperatures at around 40°C (104°F) and even in normal circumstances they will have a slightly lower internal body temperature at night than during the day. Their bodies are very efficient at changing food

22

into body fat quickly, but it is equally important that every device is used to insulate the body against outside cold and the resultant heat loss. When it is roosting a bird can do several things itself to help conserve heat. It can tuck its head under its wing or draw its feet and legs up into its feathers to reduce loss from legs, face and bill, or can avoid exposing one leg altogether by standing only on the other one: the unfeathered parts of the body are the areas which lose heat most rapidly. Feathers are the principle form of insulation of course and must be kept in tiptop condition at all time. Their insulating properties are impressive and when fluffed out they will trap a thick cushion of warm air all around the body; ninety-five per cent of the volume of a bird's plumage is air. So long as the bird keeps still and does not disturb this warm surrounding layer the heat loss will be minimised. If a cold wind is blowing however this layer is constantly disturbed and literally blown away as we can readily experience ourselves.

A good bird garden must contain sufficient cover in the form of dense evergreens, secret crevices and sheltered corners to provide a host of alternative roosting sites to meet the needs of as many species as possible. Blackbirds and song thrushes prefer to roost in thick shrubbery, often singly but occasionally with a partner, and sometimes they will make use of last year's nest for the purpose. Mistle thrushes can reveal their night time refuge in conifers, high hedges or evergreens by a lot of noisy chattering and churring before they retreat for the night; they will probably roost in small groups in early winter but by February they are sleeping singly or in pairs. Redwings and fieldfares roost in gatherings of several hundred or more in scrub woodland, evergreen shrubbery or tall hedges and not usually in gardens unless they are very large ones. The coal tit may well work its way into a thick cluster of growing conifer needles while blue tits will roost singly in any suitable crevice they can find – gaps under the eaves, the end of scaffolding pipes, nest boxes and similar. In some old houses they seem to operate a harmonious time-share arrangement with the local bats which use tiny crevices in the summer and vacate them to let the blue tits take over in autumn. At night-time dunnocks and robins retreat into the

Redwing: body feathers fluffed out for insulation against the bitter winter cold.

thick cover of greenery and the house sparrows will resort to a tangle of ivy, the depths of tall shrubbery or evergreen creepers on the house wall. Woodpeckers carve out special roosting cavities in soft decaying trees in autumn rather than used soiled holes which have been occupied by nesting birds in summer. Other species – starlings, corvids and some of the finches will remain daily commuters departing to and from the garden in late afternoon for out-of-town dormitories elsewhere.

The very smallest birds have the greatest problems. As dusk approaches the family parties of long-tailed tits fly silently – still in Indian file – into thick hawthorns or other bushes and there they roost clustered close together in a tight ball, tails outward to keep each other warm; the colder the night the tighter the huddle will be. There is suspicion that goldcrests will gather in similar groups and wrens are well known for communal roosting when weather is very cold. Until the onset of cold weather they roost individually in any variety of holes and cavities. They occupy 'cock' nests in which no broods were reared in summer or the nests of other species including long-tailed tit, swallow and house martin but find many other places too such as cavities among old ivy stems, cattle sheds and stables, holes in thatch or disused nest boxes. They are very active and quite noisy at dusk and there is often a lot of apparent consideration and inspection of alternatives before a site is eventually selected. In a cold snap wrens will lead each other to a good communal roost site and on occasions quite prodigious numbers have been found roosting together, thirty is not rare and as many as fifty have been found roosting in tiers inside one nest box!

So, keep as many potential roost sites as possible in the garden; leave a gap where roosting birds can slip into the garden shed or outhouse, don't remove old birds nests prematurely (but make sure nesting boxes are cleaned out) and the garden will become a genuine dormitory and not just a day time fast-food takeaway.

Groups of long-tailed tits huddle together to conserve heat in their winter roost.

Winter water

Drinking water is essential to garden birds throughout the year and in cold weather when birds are encouraged into the garden and rely on the regular supply of food provided we have a particular responsibility to ensure that fresh water is available too. All birds need water for drinking but especially the grain and seed eaters such as chaffinch, greenfinch, linnet, house sparrow and collared dove which need up to about ten per cent of their body weight in water each day. When the weather is warm starling, song thrush, blackbird, dunnock and blue tit are all thirsty drinkers. Birds feeding on more succulent foods such as fats, berries, invertebrates and vegetable materials are able to make use of the water content in these items but will still need to supplement it by direct drinking. Because the bird's body is covered in feathers this water is then lost, not through sweating as it is in mammals, but mainly through the high moisture content of the droppings.

Even if you have a garden pond it is going to be difficult to keep it ice-free in hard weather and it may be simpler in the end to make separate winter provision. There are many proprietory brands of bird bath and drinking device on the market, many of which are admirable. However, beware some of the vast selection of 'bird baths' on offer in garden centres which may include unsuitable (and expensive) ornamental creations often made of slippery plastic with steep sides and deep bottoms which will avalanche an unsuspecting bird into the depths of a watery hell. Bearing these considerations in mind you can select the item of your fancy ranging from moulded fibreglass receptacles at ground level, to pedestal baths or ornate designer creations guarded by gnomes, improbable storks or herons. The main thing is that they should give easy access for the birds to drink – gently sloping edges and non-slippery material. There is no need for anything elaborate and a functional do-it-yourself arrangement will suffice equally well. However if you choose to buy, the RSPB offers a simulated stone finish bath in fibreglass.

An idea that is widely canvassed and which works well is an upturned dustbin lid sunk into the ground or otherwise propped up level. The great problem in winter is keeping the water unfrozen. You may be at home all the time and can run out with endless kettles of warm water, but it's a bit too labour-intensive for most and a better solution has to be sought. If you employ the dustbin lid method it is a good idea to lift it up onto some bricks, create a sheltered cavity and put a little

Dustbin lid and heater.

slow-burning nightlight under it. Alternatively, whatever type of drinking bath you have you can fairly easily install a small water heater to maintain the temperature above freezing point. An ordinary aquarium heater with a submerged thermostat will do the job admirably but if you are using any electrical device in water it is essential to have it fitted by a properly qualified electrician who can ensure that both for your sake and the birds, the electrical power is confined to the heater! These heaters are nowadays very reliable and, properly installed, perfectly safe for outside use. What you should never do is to use any form of antifreeze, glycerine or salt in the water as this could be extremely harmful to the birds themselves and will risk damage to their feathers when they preen after bathing. Bathing is the second vital reason why birds need water and they must bathe regularly even in the depths of winter to ensure that their feathers are kept in first class condition and work efficiently as insulation as well as for flight (bathing is dealt with more fully in a later section).

Keep the drinking water fresh because birds will continually dirty it by bathing in it, and change it whenever necessary. Not only do birds prefer clean water but it will help prevent the drinking bath becoming soiled and a potential catchpit for diseases. As with other garden bird devices try to make sure that it is not too close to cover where cats can lurk and pounce.

Rapacious starlings

Every year several million starlings invade the lowlands of Britain when they flee the advancing grip of winter in continental Europe. Including our own resident birds the total wintering here may reach upwards of forty million. It sometimes seems that most of them spend the time in our particular garden and it is difficult to believe that a hundred years or more ago the starling was an uncommon bird in much of Britain. In fact most of the daily raiding parties which come out from the huge night-time roosts to loot the bird table are usually no more than fifty strong although their bustle, aggression and pillaging make them appear like a barbarian army. The roosts, which may on occasion contain as many as a million birds, are usually in conifer plantations or dense shrubbery; in towns and cities we are all familiar with the developed habit of roosting on the high ledges of buildings. The noisy pre-roost assemblies and swirling synchronous clouds of starlings above the roost site are one of the spectacular sights of winter birdwatching.

The winter starling is an omnivorous feeder which subsists extensively on invertebrates from pastureland, playing fields and lawns when the ground is soft but also profits from the inexhaustible stockpiles of food available at man-made supply centres such as farmyards, bird tables, rubbish tips and sewage farms. Life is easier for starlings in winter than for any other garden bird.

At the bird table the starlings are tough customers dominating the space to the exclusion of others and fighting, bickering and squabbling noisily amongst themselves. Any food on offer is fair game and they can reduce a well provisioned table to a bare larder in next to no time. Although they are first and foremost ground feeders they will readily move onto the elevated bird table and even show considerable dexterity and resourcefulness in using hanging bird feeders. Most people's

Hawfinch drinking: birds, especially seed eaters, need regular access to drinking water.

Starlings are rowdy and aggressive feeders which dominate feeding sites to the exclusion of more shy birds. Deterring them is possible but they are also entertaining and amusing visitors.

interest in starlings at the garden feeding station revolves around how to keep them at bay and prevent them devouring everything that is put out. People tend to have a healthy dislike for starlings which is unfortunate because, apart from their deficient table manners and slightly unsavoury roost sites, they are actually engaging birds. They have beautiful iridescent plumage and amusing habits and are one of the world's most universal and successful species.

How to deter starlings is a difficult question and one which has no simple answer. Bread is one of the least nutritious bulk foods regularly used in the garden but when put out on the ground in any quantity starlings will quickly exploit it and it can then have the advantage of helping to deflect them from other foods. Some people will go to the trouble of surrounding the bird table itself with wire mesh to exclude starlings but it is slightly tiresome and makes restocking, cleaning and operating the bird table fiddly. It also simultaneously excludes blackbird, song thrush and other welcome feeders of similar size. Starlings are some of the last arrivals most mornings – the roost is probably several miles away – so try to put food out very early to give the smaller and shier species

the chance to stock up before the flying squads arrive. Similarly wait until the starlings fly off in flocks in the early afternoon before topping up the table again. Starling and house sparrow – another numerous visitor with unquenchable hunger and wasteful habits – are both fairly wary species and can sometimes be persuaded to a subsidiary feeding area separate from your 'prime' one and a bit farther away from the house if the layout of your garden allows it and the level of wholesale pilfering demands. Window-sill tables, for example, are usually too close to the house for comfort for the starling.

Hoarding food

Most birds coming to the winter bird table use it with reasonable decorum as a self-service restaurant where they can satisfy their immediate needs. A few species however will extend the invitation by regarding it as a take-away stall. One or two larger birds such as black-headed gull, magpie or carrion crow may be bold enough to make lightening strikes to snatch a beakful and make off to a safer distance to eat it, but they are not hoarders. The real hoarders work with a lower profile

*Jays are skilful nest finders in spring and summer. In
autumn they collect large numbers of acorns which they
hide for winter use.*

Coal tits will make repeated visits to feeders, taking food items away to hoard them for future use.

but with methodical application and dedicated perseverance. They will return time and again, especially the early part of the day, and fly off with peanuts or other choice morsels which they hide away to recover later in the day, or even on subsequent days.

Principal among these hoarders are the nuthatch and the coal tit. The nuthatch is dominant among other small birds at the table and its visits are thus fairly unrestricted. It particularly selects peanuts to remove and hoard and can be watched repeatedly coming to the feeder, prising out a peanut and taking it off into nearby trees or woodland to hide it. Coal tits are more circumspect and being fairly low down the pecking order at the bird table have to wait their time, avoiding the melee and slipping in quietly to take a morsel of fat or fragment of peanut when things are quieter. Once you know these two species regularly raid the feeders to remove items to stash away it is easy to watch their different strategies to achieve it. Both of course store wild foods too; nuthatches hide beechmast, acorns or hazel nuts and coal tits remove conifer seeds but also insect larvae – which they incapacitate but don't kill presumably because they keep longer alive – and little pellets of aphids stuck together with saliva. They tuck the morsels away in crevices in bark, hidden in moss, grass, tussocks and similar places while nuthatches hide most of theirs in crevices in trunks and branches. Such a strategy of food storage is only as good as the bird's memory for relocating the hiding places and it has been shown that most birds do in fact recover a high percentage of the items they hide: presumably they use favourite hiding places regularly which will help. This habit of hoarding is one which coal tits practice throughout the year with the exception of the breeding season and the cold spells in winter, both of which are times when they need all the food they can obtain for immediate consumption. At other times of year twenty-five per cent of the day may be spent in collecting food for storage.

Marsh tit and willow tit also both store food items and although they are less regular in visiting the bird table for that purpose, especially the willow tit, if you are lucky enough to have either species as a regular visitor you will be able to detect them as food hoarders. Winter survival is all about resourcefulness and the great tit, which does not hoard food itself will sometimes latch on to the fact that these smaller birds are hiding food items and will follow them to steal the spoils as soon as the owner's back is turned.

Among the larger birds the jay is a major hoarder of food and in autumn spends a great deal of time collecting acorns and burying them in leaf litter, in soft ground in bramble patches or under dead bracken. This is an operation of big proportions and in good acorn years prodigious numbers are transported and buried for retrieval in the winter and spring, an exercise which is necessary simply because acorns are the jays staple food, but in autumn they are also quickly used up by woodpigeons, rooks and a host of other acorn eaters. In years, such as 1983, when the acorn crop totally fails we may see large autumn movements of jays as they move away in search of food. The jay is wily enough to have learned too that in spring and summer it is rewarding to pull the new green oak seedlings to retrieve the acorn attached to the bottom, although it will ignore the slightly bigger brown saplings which have already used up the acorn food.

Private courtship of the robin

The robin is one of the most belligerent of garden birds, a born pugilist unprepared to tolerate its own kind at any time of year except for a chosen mate during the breeding season. All through the autumn and winter both males and females have kept fiercely independent territories, agreeing neutral zones only at feeding and drinking stations. In late winter it becomes very difficult for

29

both the cock and hen birds, who now have to overcome the strong instinct to repel another robin on sight, to set about accepting a mate. For the male bird a strange robin now has to be accepted in his territory while at the same time all other individuals still have to be kept out. At first it is very difficult for the male to adjust to this new situation and the birds which have been best at repulsing intruders all winter will show the greatest initial aggression to hens even though they are simultaneously singing to attract them!

Tradition touchingly claims that robin pairs are normally formed around St Valentine's day, which is a pleasant thought although the process probably begins earlier than that most years. On the mild days of mid-winter the male robin starts to sing his spring song to advertise for a mate and in response to this a female will eventually fly into his territory. The cock instinctively postures aggressively and the female will then respond defensively in the same manner. He will move away – doubtless in confusion – as the foundations of his isolationism begin to crumble. Then he will sing again, a short phrase or two from another song post; she too may sing a little and then follow him again and slowly the masque unfolds as the performance is repeated and more encores are called. It may not all happen in one day but steadily the aggression of the cock dissipates until the point is reached at which his isolation finally gives way to the stronger impulses of the breeding season; the mate is accepted and the pair bond formed.

Despite the fact that the robin is such a familiar and well-loved garden bird, this aspect of its behaviour is difficult to see. Robins are early risers, often the first to be on the move well before daylight proper, and this very private part of the robin's life is usually carried out discreetly in the half light at the beginning of the day.

Nuthatches are great hoarders of individual food items and remarkably successful at retrieving them later.

MARCH

Mistle thrush – the March bird

The mistle thrush is a real March bird. In the very earliest days of the month its far-carrying challenging song from high in the windy tree tops is a herald of coming spring. It has been singing since the turn of the year on mild days but now it is constant and insistent: even the wildest March days do not drown the passion of the 'storm cock'. The roving family bands of mistle thrushes broke up in autumn when individual birds and established pairs started to defend selected supplies of winter fruit from all others. Throughout the winter they must protect this source or survival is in the balance. To illustrate the point it is clear that most of the young birds fail to find an assured and defensible fruit supply and they migrate south to France leaving the older, experienced birds in command of winter stocks. Mistletoe is a favourite food – thus the bird's name – but it depends heavily on yew, rowan, holly, hawthorn and ivy as mistletoe is now much scarcer than it used to be because so many of the orchard apple trees on which it grows have now been grubbed out.

The mistle thrush nests early and in mild winters may have eggs by early March. Try an open box-tray about 6 in (15 cm) square and 4 in (10 cm) deep in the high crotch of an old apple or other tall tree. You may be lucky and have them nest there but they are not short of natural nest sites. They defend big territories in the breeding season, up to several acres in size, and protect them with boldness and vigour. They are extremely aggressive in their boundary disputes and fearless in pursuit of ground or airborne predators which dare to go anywhere near the nest. The March mistle thrush is both a conspicuous and formidable guardsman.

The fight for territory

Our resident garden blackbirds have maintained loosely-held territories all through the long winter. These territories are probably closely in line with those which they defended for the breeding season last year. As March progresses they become much more assertive and aggressive towards each other as the territories are consolidated and the boundaries proclaimed; the up-and-coming, first time adults vie to fill the vacancies left by winter deaths or try to force an additional territory in between established ones. There is actually a lot more stability in most of these territory boundaries year by year than might be imagined. Traditional territories frequently centre on a particularly good nest site – albeit a new nest is built each year – in a certain thicket or dense patch of shrubbery which has been used in successive years; a series of old nests in one small area often gives evidence to this and the pattern is particularly strong in many suburban areas.

So now, through March, there is much chasing and posturing among the male blackbirds, a lot of sitting on visible prominences and energetic singing. Singing males often prefer to use one favourite, high-elevation song post and suburban blackbirds in particular have no shortage of chim-

In winter experienced mistle thrushes remain strongly territorial, each bird defending its own exclusive fruit supply.

ney pots, roof tops, lamp posts, TV aerials and telegraph poles to choose from.

Song thrushes started to re-establish their territories as long ago as last autumn and individual birds of both sexes will probably have held territories through the winter. Now this pattern of holdings has to be revised and since mid-winter – interrupted only by cold spells of weather – the male song thrush has been gradually increasing the tempo of his singing; now, in mid-March he is in full voice. This spring song is full of passion and vigour and is the song thrush's declaration of ownership.

Experienced male chaffinches similarly return to the same territory year after year and when their neighbours do the same the boundaries will change remarkably little. In February the males were present on site only during the mornings but now as the pressure on space increases they will stay all day. Young male chaffinches trying to establish territory for the first time make a later entry than the old birds and thus incur a double handicap – inexperience and a late start. When the young male bird finds a site which is apparently vacant he is extremely nervous and tentative to start with, calling gently and singing in short sub-songs before he gradually gains confidence in the absence of competition with the passing days and graduates to conspicuous song perches and eventually full song. Boundary skirmishes with neighbours will follow and may be fierce as the young bird learns the hard way about observing the rules of others' hard-won boundaries. These differences in behaviour of young and old birds can be clearly seen once you know what to look for.

None of our other breeding finches has a territorial imperative equal to the chaffinch. All the other garden nesters – bullfinch, greenfinch, goldfinch, linnet and hawfinch are either non-territorial (bullfinch) or loosely colonial (goldfinch) in their nesting and defend only very small territories immediately around the nest itself. They breed in loose groups and often have to travel considerable distances away from the nests to collect food. The pair formation is never as strongly defined with these birds as it is with the chaffinch (they may often feed in groups for example which breeding chaffinches will never do), and one result of this is that none compares with the chaffinch as a songster. Bullfinch and hawfinch offer the merest apologies of song, a dubious distinction they share with only one other of our garden birds, the spotted flycatcher. The jingling conversational song of goldfinches is unmistakable, as is the wheezing song of the greenfinch invariably delivered from the very top of a tall tree. One or two of the finches have singing display flights but they are little used with the exception of the greenfinch which has a distinctive, slow-flapping 'bat-flight' in which the males weave slowly around the tree tops, singing as they do so and displaying bright yellow patches on wings and tail.

Inevitably some birds will simply fail to establish a breeding territory for one reason or another. In some parts of the country (eg Wales) carrion crows are so numerous that all the available space is taken up and non-breeders have to remain in flocks; male great tits outnumber females and thus not all succeed in finding a mate and holding territory. As ever it is the young who are the luckless ones. Holding territory and attracting a mate are the keys to success in the breeding season. Once again there is little which is left to chance, and experience pays every time. It is the 'wise old birds' who are in pole position for the breeding season stakes. Now, in the weeks before the first waves of migrants arrive to set up summer homes, most of our resident birds have already got their act together and the pattern for the season is set.

Siskins at peanuts

In many ways the siskin is an unlikely client at the garden feeders. This beautiful little yellow-and-green finch is an inhabitant of conifer woods during the breeding season where its fine pointed bill is specially designed to extract seeds from the cones of spruce, fir, pine and larch. Its nests, high in the outer branches of tall conifers, are exceptionally difficult to spot. If you are fortunate enough to have siskins breeding near you it is quite likely that when the family parties come out of the conifer woods in July and August they may venture down to feed on the seed heads of dandelion, thistle, knapweed and dock. If your garden offers this possibility keep a good rough area of these weeds to lure the siskins. If you can't entice the siskins at least the goldfinches will thank you for them. When the cones have emptied their seeds in mid-summer the siskins leave their breeding woods in search of an alternative diet – an autumn fare of birch seeds, and later alder will sustain them through the winter. In the 1960's siskins in several parts of Britain discovered the fat put out in feeders for tits and the habit of visiting garden bird tables rapidly developed and spread. Nowadays in late winter and early spring rural and even suburban gardens in many areas are regularly visited by parties of siskins. They have developed a predeliction for peanuts, especially when supplied in the common *red* mesh bags. Why they have this preference for red bags is a mystery but in any case it is not a rigid or universal preference and sometimes they will come as readily to other types of hanging feeder. To show how perverse they can be in some gardens they will shun red mesh bags in preference to other hanging feeders! So evidently we still have a lot to learn about siskins at our feeding table although to be fair one supposes that siskins themselves are still evolving their relationship with feeding stations. It is a habit which only started about twenty years ago and already they are exploiting other foods in addition to hanging fat and peanuts; they will take seeds, cheese and cereal-based foods as well. Siskins show commendable aggression for such small birds and can hold their own well at the feeders. They are a little inconsistent in their attendance from one year to another, probably depending on the availability of wild food, but they are certainly one of the most attractive and engaging small birds that you can attract to the garden.

Male greenfinches have a slow, weaving bat-like flight among the tree tops as part of their courtship display.

Chaffinches are aggressive when setting up territory; some aggression may even be shown to partners in the early stages of courtship and pair formation.

The attractive siskin is increasingly making use of garden feeding areas in late winter.

A robin cocks its head to look, not listen, for worms on the lawn.

Lawns

An open well-kept lawn is almost essential to a good bird garden. It is a trysting ground for blackbirds and pigeons and the largest open area you have on which to watch the garden birds. It is an ideal hunting area for birds which feed on ants, leatherjackets, small spiders and grubs, but above all a good lawn is a non-stop conveyor belt of juicy, nutritious earthworms. In spring starlings probe for worms moving energetically about the lawn, and they rely heavily on this diet for a few weeks when they are coming into breeding condition. Robin, song thrush and blackbird are the most skilled exponents of the worm catch, watching with heads cocked to one side before they pounce on the hidden prey. We humans cock our head on one side to listen more carefully; birds do it to focus a gimlet eye on the minute movement of the ground where the worm is. The saying that 'it is the early bird that catches the worm' is a very accurate observation of fact because the worms are active in the moist and cool of night-time and the dewey dawn. Once the sun is up and the warmth caresses the surface they retreat well underground again.

Earthworm numbers are highest in spring and summer and they are often maligned by those who are lawn-proud but their usefulness should never be overlooked. They are crucial to the well-kept lawn, aerating, draining and fertilising it and the worm casts they throw up on the surface are a small price to pay for such an indispensable service. If you see these casts as unsightly or annoying at mowing time spread them with a lawn rake but do not use worm killer because you will do yourself and your lawn a disservice as well as depriving birds — and hedgehogs, shrews and other mammals — of an important source of food.

The larger the lawn you can create, the better. It will provide you with a good clear arena in which to watch the birds and may well help you to site the bird table or other feeders well out in the open and away from lurking cats. These larger lawns will also help to provide space for shier birds such as song thrush and dunnock which prefer to feed away from the hurly-burly around the bird table. In mid-summer green woodpeckers may be visitors to the lawn to hunt for ants (and many people are briefly duped into believing that they have a golden oriole!). Unseen by us the harvest of worms is still exploited at night; crepuscular little owls take many and if your lawn is very large and is near woodland, who knows but that woodcock may feed there silently and regularly in the depth of night?

So, look after the bird-garden lawn well. Rake it and feed it if you need to but keep it well mown because long grass is of little use to birds. By removing all the cuttings we do of course deprive the lawn of many of the very nutrients it needs to ensure that it flourishes. Continual cutting with no feeding will impoverish the soil and deplete the lawn's community of worms and other invertebrates.

Trees

The presence of trees in the bird garden is one of the most important elements of your garden plan. Birds use trees for a variety of purposes — refuge, feeding, nesting, roosting and as song posts and look out perches. Early March is an ideal time for planting your chosen trees now that the ground is drying out and the soil temperature is warming up, but before new spring growth becomes vigorous. This is a job which must be thought about carefully because it will be many years before the trees are fully mature and once planted they are there for good so there is really only one chance to get it right. One of the first decisions you should make is whether you are going to plant native trees which will be rich in bird food, both insects and fruits, or exotics which may give you more attractive colours and shapes. Flowering cherries, locust trees and beautiful magnolias may be highly decorative but bring little by way of return for

Bird trees for the garden

(Maximum heights given in brackets)

Forest giants – don't plant these unless you have a giant garden!

Ash (80 ft/24.4 m) (*Fraxinus exelcior*) Popular look-out and song posts. Ash keys provide winter food, especially for bull-finches.

Beech (100 ft/30.5 m) (*Fagus sylvatica*) Beech mast is *the* major winter food for many garden birds. Massive form and total shade.

Oak (80 ft/24.4 m) (*Quercus robor, Q. petraea*) Single most important wildlife tree – fruits and insects for feeding, abundant nest sites. Huge, spreading form.

Hornbeam (80 ft/24.4 m) (*Carpinus betulus*) Greenfinches and hawfinches love winter seeds. Unfortunately hawfinches prefer trees in groups, rather than singly!

Deciduous natives

Alder (60 ft/18.3 m) (*Alnus glutinosa*) Wet sites. Insect rich and woodpeckers, tits, treecreeper, warblers and redpoll, siskin and others feed on winter seed cones.

Aspen (70 ft/21.3 m) (*Populus tremula*) Quick-growing, insect rich – suits warblers and tits especially. Light shade; attractive 'trembling' leaves.

Birch (60 ft/18.3 m) (*Betula pendula, B.pubesceus*) Another 'top drawer' bird tree: insects and seeds. Redpolls and others feed on spring catkins. Woodpeckers and willow tits nest in decaying stumps. Quick growing; light shade.

Elder (20 ft/6 m) (*Sambucus nigra*) Not often considered for planting but a good wildlife tree. Flowers attract many insects, birds love autumn elderberries. Flowers and berries are winemaker's delight!

Hazel (20 ft/6 m) (*Corylus avellana*) Hazel nuts are important winter food for birds and mammals. Another insect-rich tree: good bird feeding.

Hawthorn (20 ft/6 m) (*Cratagus monogyna, C. oxycanthoides*) Boy-proof hedgerow plant but also makes a good standard. A key bird tree for all-year insects and winter berries. Much used for thorny nest sites.

Larch (80 ft/24.4 m) (*Larix decidua*) Use for quick-growing shelter on a bare site. Good seed producer.

Rowan and whitebeam (50 ft/15.2 m) (*Sorbus aucuparia, S. aria*) Attractive white flowers, light shade, heavy autumn berry crop. Quick growing; both produce berries early in life.

Wild cherry (70 ft/21.3 m) (*Prunus avium*) Grows to very big tree. Good nest sites; popular summer fruit crop for birds.

Willows (*Salix spp*) Many species; all first class for birds. Avoid larger species. Pussy willow (*Salix caprea*) has everything to commend it – size, shape, amenable to pruning, earliest flowers and masses of seed in autumn. Warblers, tits, gold-crests make a bee-line for it.

Native evergreens

Holly (50 ft/15.2 m) (*Ilex aquifolium*) An important tree – nest sites, roosting, insect food and mid-winter berries. Berries only on female trees; male tree needed for pollination.

Scots pine (80 ft/24.4 m) (*Pinus sylvaticus*) Too big for most gardens. Good for corvid nests; owls. Rich insect fauna; pine cones for crossbills.

Juniper (15 ft/4.6 m) (*Juniper communis*) Good native with popular berries for birds and good nesting shelter. Innumerable varieties now available, choose to suit needs, but ensure it will have berries.

Non-native evergreens – speedy short-term shelter.

Lawson cypress (60 ft/18.3 m) (*Chamaecyparis lawsoniana*) Tightly columnar. Many varieties: 'Elwoodii' (bluish) is good for small gardens. Nesting for dunnock, thrushes, goldfinch. Good roosting and pinnacle song post for chaffinch and greenfinch.

Leyland cypress (50 ft/15.2 m) (*Cypressocyparis leylandii*) Fastest grower bar none. Rapid shelter and nest sites. Good wind-proof hedge; cut to height. Castigated as suburban take-over plant but has good bird uses.

birds. The best bird interest lies in native British trees which have their own myriad communities of edible insects and autumn fruits. Some of these natives hold truly prodigious numbers of insects, both in quantity and diversity: oak may support over 300 species, willow 250, birch 225, hawthorn 150 and poplar 100.

When selecting the species which you decide are most appropriate for your garden it is important to bear several other considerations in mind. Make sure you know the eventual size and form of the trees because many can grow very large and will cast heavy shade in years to come, as they mature. The space they will eventually occupy is not easy to visualise at this stage. Ensure that both your soil type and the size and nature of your garden are suitable for the trees you are intending; your local nurseryman will advise you on these points. It is sensible to take note of the trees that are already growing nearby as it is pointless to duplicate unnecessarily if you could encourage more birds by adding to the tree selection which already exists around your garden. Remember that however small your garden is there are good bird trees available to suit it. Use the table on page 37 as a guide and take further advice from your nurseryman.

The table lists those trees which are particularly useful for garden birds. Several familiar woodland species are not included because they are either of limited use for birds (even though they may be of interest for other garden wildlife) eg sycamore, horse chestnut, lime, maple, or because they have features which make them inappropriate for planting in conventional gardens eg black poplar. Similarly elm is sadly left off in view of the fact the Dutch elm disease is still ravaging the species throughout England and Wales and it has to be inappropriate to suggest planting new ones until the problem is resolved. If you have elms in the garden hedgerow, leave as much of the dead timber as you safely can, or at least the stumps, and allow them to regenerate as scrub and then cut back as necessary so that you are effectively coppicing at intervals. Elm is a very important wildlife tree, not least for birds, and its loss is a sad one.

Spring arrivals

March at last sees the return of the first summer visitors, home-coming from their winter season in the sun. Although each year there are a few aberrant individuals which arrive even earlier, it is in the second week of this month that the earliest arrivals normally appear. The first two to reach the headlands and cliffs of the south coast are the ring ouzel and wheatear. Neither of these are regular garden birds (unless your garden is on Beachy Head, the Norfolk coast or the high flanks of the Pennines) and they will immediately push on farther north towards their breeding grounds in the hills once they have rested from the sea crossing and fed for a short while. Both are night migrants and therefore they can rest and feed during the day of arrival before moving on the following night. They have wintered in the Mediterranean basin and therefore are relatively short-distance migrants compared to many of the other birds which will form the main tide of arrivals in April and early May. Another small bird which has wintered in the Mediterranean area and arrives about a week after the first wheatears is the chiffchaff. This is a regular garden visitor in early spring and will feed non-stop on whatever midges and hidden aphids it can find among the buds of pussy willow, alder, poplar and other trees, pausing only to repeat its cheery song time and time again – chiff,chaff,chiff,chiff,chaff,chiff,chaff. It is the first real herald of spring in the garden and a song more than welcome for that reason.

At about the same time as the chiffchaff appears, the first long-distance migrant, the sand martin, arrives. It has wintered in West Africa and has had to make the hazardous crossing of the western Sahara before crossing the Mediterranean, Iberia and France. Many sand martins winter in the barren Sahel region south of the Sahara which has suffered continuous drought for many years now and their numbers are now much reduced because of the desertification that is taking place in their traditional winter home.

Each of these species, like all our other summer passerine visitors, are insect eaters and the cold windy days of late March must frequently be difficult times for these birds which rely entirely on the emergence of insects in warm sunny weather. Spring may be here but the chiffchaffs probably take some convincing.

Smartening up the spring plumage

As the breeding season approaches the regular garden visitors are developing a brighter plumage week by week. It is easy to see that it is occurring, but how do they manage to do it when the complete feather moult took place last summer and will not happen again until the forthcoming season has passed? The answer is that on many

The goldcrest is one of several small insectivorous birds which find rich feeding on sallows.

birds the new feathers produced by moulting have pale tips which obscure some of the colour lower down. These tips slowly abrade during the course of a winter so that by the time the breeding season arrives the adult birds have revealed their brightest colours in time for courtship and display. The tips of these feathers are weaker than the remainder and they wear down to expose the colour below throughout the year, but especially so immediately after the moult in September and October and again before the breeding season, in March and April.

Notice now how brilliantly coloured the great tits have become; the bold black stripe down the belly is much broader on the male than that on the female and the black-and-white pattern on the head is more defined. Blue tits too have clean, crisp colours and even the more subtle shades of the treecreeper, dunnock and house sparrow have brightened. Bill colour too can change. The young male blackbird will develop his golden yellow bill

in the first winter and will then retain it. Chaffinches however have a horn-coloured bill in winter which becomes blue for the breeding season and then reverts. It is amazing what a few special hormones can do in spring.

Courtship and display

Once the male birds have beaten the bounds of their new breeding territory the priority turns to attracting a mate. Song is just as important for this purpose as it is in the setting up of territory and it is the means by which the male advertises his presence and invites the attention of the hen. Once she has come to his territory he will use his full repertoire of displays and posturing to entice her to stay; thereafter he must continue to cement the bond.

This is the time when birds can look at their most impressive but also their most ridiculous. In full courtship the blackbird adopts a striking and

The chaffinch's bill changes from horn-coloured to blue at the onset of the breeding season.

The male blackbird's somewhat undistinguished courtship takes place on the open lawn, often in the early morning.

improbable pose in which the rump feathers are fluffed out, the head is stretched right forward and the feathers on the crown elevated, crest-like. With tail fanned and bill open he displays to the female making bowing movements and short 'rodent' runs towards her while simultaneously warbling in strangled *sotto voce* phrases. This somewhat undignified display duly impresses his mate despite her apparent studied indifference.

Chaffinch pairs are together for several weeks before nesting begins. Across this period the courtship intensifies and a strange and unusual transfer of power slowly takes place. As in other conventional bird courtships, it is the male who initiates affairs although as time passes it is the female who will eventually become the dominant partner. The cock postures to make himself sleek and slender and maximise the effects of his smart white wing chevrons; he tilts sideways to elevate one wing and display the bright red flank and belly. Like the female blackbird his mate appears unimpressed and so he may try a different tactic, leading her on around the territory with an enticing 'moth-flight' of shallow, rapid wing beats. As she grows in confidence in his territory she becomes more assertive and loses her fear of the cock, even attacking him in between his continuing bouts of courtship until the final balance of their partnership is achieved with the male firmly put in his place. This female dominance will then

Male willow warblers give an attractive slow wing-waving display to the females.

help ensure her priority of feeding at the time she needs to form the eggs.

The ebullient starling, whose defended territory surprisingly extends only about one yard from its nest hole, depends mainly on the persuasiveness and passion of his song. When a female lands nearby he will move to the nest hole and redouble his singing and wing-quivering in a frenzy devised to attract her to inspect the premises. Sexual chases, often well away from the nest, will follow and once the pair is formed and a nest is built the solicitous male will decorate the nest with fresh greenery and often the bright flowers of celandine, polyanthus, daisy, bluebell or daffodil. But like some other inconstant males, once the pair bond is well founded the supply of bouquets dries up and the female starling, forsaken and flowerless, will often then gather her own.

Willow warblers will sing immediately they arrive and once the females have joined the males courtship starts without delay. The male chases the female through the trees and when she stops he pauses too with one wing, or sometimes both, raised to start a slow wing-waving display. Willow warblers also indulge in mutual billing, occasional courtship feeding or slow 'butterfly' display flights.

Some species, including all the crows, pair for life but all the same courtship is essential as spring approaches and the pair bond must be strengthened to help the birds get into readiness for breeding. In spring the well-known gatherings of magpies — 'magpie marriages' as they are often called — have an important role in this respect.

Over gravel pits and riversides sand martins have to work hard to find enough insect food in the early days of spring.

Much displaying takes place in these groups which will move freely from territory to territory, with individual birds rising high with slow flapping before sweeping round in a wide circle in front of the mate. On the ground either cock or hen may display spontaneously to its mate with wing-flirting, bowing or tilting postures; always they will display to give maximum effect of the striking white wing patches. Female magpies will solicit food from the male and this courtship feeding, which is most frequent around egg-laying, is a powerful part of courtship and pair-bonding with many garden birds. Most species of tits will do it, with the female 'baby-begging' the male; so will most of the finches (except chaffinch), robin, thrushes (but not frequently) and some warblers.

Early nests

Increasing day length and gradually rising temperatures are the main triggers which bring birds into breeding readiness, but the availability of food and the condition of the adults are also important. Where food is abundant some pairs may imprudently lay much earlier than normal. Robin nests are not unknown in January and reasonably frequent in Frebruary; song thrushes and blackbirds mainly start to lay from late March onwards but will sometimes have early nests in mid-winter. This out-of-season nesting is most prevalent in suburban gardens where abundant food is supplied; so in mild weather at this time of year you may well be helping these garden birds to make a flying start to the season. The mistle thrush is regularly the earliest breeder among the garden birds, nests being built before the end of February most years when they often have to contend with falls of snow and severe cold.

The success of many of these unseasonal nests is poor however. It is claimed that few of the early robins produce flying young and a change of weather or predation by cats and others puts paid to many blackbirds and song thrushes before there is sufficient leaf cover to hide the nests properly.

APRIL

In spring magpies display in small groups initially before forming their pairs and setting up individual territories.

April is a month of frantic bird activity. Not only is it one of the busiest times of year for birds but it is the time when the gardener too must put in a lot of work tidying and planting the garden, repairing winter damage and generally getting the garden into good order both for himself and for birds and other garden wildlife for the remainder of the year.

Summer bird table

April is the time to adjust the amount of food you are providing on the bird table. You must decide too whether to continue providing through the spring and summer or to slowly stop altogether. Opinion is divided but in general the view is that there is no need to continue through the breeding season and the time of summer plenty: better to let the birds seek out the right natural foods especially for feeding to the young. This is certainly the advice of the RSPB who point out that birds should not become totally dependent on you for food, especially if they are likely to collect indigestable items such as peanuts or other large seeds and feed them to young. If the summer is very dry blackbirds and song thrushes which take large numbers of earthworms may have difficulty in finding food in the hard ground and there may be a case for supplementary help. Now is the time when the birds should repay you for the winter bounty, helping to keep the garden free of insect pests.

In any event, from the beginning of April it is best to reduce the amount of food you put out. Curtail the supplies of suet, fats, hemp and other high calorie foods, and avoid putting down bread which is low-value bulk and will stuff a nestling bird like wadding in a cushion if fed to it by the adults. If you do keep on feeding, limit it to carefully selected household scraps – stale cake or ground cereals – or best of all, live food such as mealworms or ant larvae. Keep it to a minimum and at least it will maintain the continuity and keep the birds tame so that by the time you increase it again in autumn the hard core will already know the ropes.

Nest sites for all

The April bird garden should be able to offer a wide choice of nest sites that will attract as many different breeding birds as possible. With good planning and an understanding of the needs of different species you can ensure that the garden is not simply a winter health-food farm but becomes a twelve-month residential suburb with a booming birth rate.

Garden birds can be divided generally into those which nest in holes and cavities and those which don't. The hole-nesting species include the following and many of them will nest almost as readily in holes in walls and buildings as they will in tree holes or nest boxes; some of course nest exclusively in non-tree holes in any case (swift, wagtails).

Birds which nest in holes:

Stock dove	
Little owl	
Tawny owl	
Swift	
Great spotted woodpecker	(excavate their own tree holes)
Pied wagtail	
Grey wagtail	
Pied flycatcher	(hill areas of the west and north)
Redstart	
Marsh tit	
Willow tit	(excavate their own nest holes in rotten stumps)
Coal tit	(frequently mouse holes or similar at ground level)
Blue tit	
Great tit	
Nuthatch	
Treecreeper	
House sparrow	(also builds its own nests in tall hedges etc)
Tree sparrow	
Starling	

Many of these birds will readily use special nest boxes and this aspect is dealt with later in the book. In addition to putting up nest boxes there is quite a lot else you can do to provide for the hole nesters. Naturally many of them prefer tree holes so if you have old fruit trees or old decaying stumps retain them if you can, or even go to the trouble of importing one or two into the garden: birch, alder or willow may be the most manageable. Don't be afraid to start off a few holes yourself with the brace and bit or power drill. Keep the hole size $1\frac{1}{4}$ in (32 mm) diameter and willow tits (low down) or woodpeckers (higher up) may take it over from you. We don't suggest that you start to undermine the fabric of the house or the outbuildings, but do not be averse to widening a few of the cracks and crevices, at least large enough to let a blue tit, redstart or nuthatch explore the possibilities if they wish. In the west of Britain redstarts frequently make use of holes in such places, especially in stone buildings where the lime mortar is old and powdery. If you build a wall in the garden leave plenty of gaps and holes in it. Drill through the outer skin of the breeze-blocks in the garage wall in the shelter of the roof overhang

Jackdaws are one of the species of garden predators which will watch human visits to nest sites and thus learn where the nests are located.

— the big cavity inside is a gift for great tits or blue tits! Grey wagtails will love any cavity well above water level on the masonry of a bridge or retaining wall alongside a stream or mill leat and pied wagtails will readily occupy equivalent sites further away from water. So enjoy yourself with the drill and the cold chisel; making holes is good fun so long as you know when to stop.

There is a group of birds which like to nest indoors and will appreciate easy access to the garage, wood shed, garden shed or stables. Wrens, robins and blackbirds frequently take up such opportunities and swallows depend on them. They build their nests against beams and rafters, or sometimes lodged on fittings against the wall. Once they have adopted you they will return each year so long as you leave the window or door open for them. Pied wagtails often nest in open fronted sheds too and they, together with robin, wren and spotted flycatcher may be persuaded to choose open-fronted nest boxes, although the flycatcher will as happily use a ledge in the porch, an upturned coconut shell against the wall or a level site on the mature stems of creepers.

Hedges and shrubberies are the obvious natural places for nest sites of those species which do not nest in cavities. Hawthorn, holly, yew and beech make the best hedges in this respect and contain plenty of likely building sites as well as providing good barriers against disturbance and predation. Hazel, on the other hand, is poor because it has few crotches and forks. Prune or clip your hedge in the early spring or autumn and avoid doing it during the breeding season if you can as it is all too easy to expose a nest inside or cause the birds to desert. Several of the exotic conifers frequently grown in our gardens offer very good nesting cover (see page 37) and require very little managing. If you have a tall overgrown hedge it may well provide a second floor site for magpie, woodpigeon, turtle dove or collared dove.

Birds which regularly nest in hedges, trees and shrubbery in the garden:

Collared dove	Whitethroat
Turtle dove	Lesser whitethroat
Wood pigeon	Goldcrest
Dunnock	Thrushes
Garden warbler	Finches
Blackcap	Magpie
Chiffchaff	

One or two additional garden breeders do not fit comfortably into any of the above categories. The cuckoo of course builds no nest of its own but exploits those of dunnock or robin. Robins, willow

46

warblers and yellowhammers nest at ground level in rank grass or hedge bottom if your garden is large. If there are really big trees in the garden you may have carrion crow or rook nesting.

Somewhere in the country there must be the ultimate bird house, a human home that is bowed down under the weight of breeding birds! Jackdaws in the chimney, swifts, starlings and house sparrows in the roof, a colony of house martins under the eaves, wren, robin, blackbird and song thrush in the creepers around the walls and spotted flycatcher and swallows on the ledges in the porch; in such a house there would have to be blue tits and a pair of wagtails in nest boxes on the wall and probably chaffinches in the honeysuckle over the porch. That's fourteen species. Surely someone somewhere could claim to have at least twelve different species actually on or in the house?

Finally, remember that all these nesting sites are constantly at risk. Adult birds are more vulnerable in the breeding season than at almost any other time of year because then they are obliged to stay in one fixed spot. Jays, magpies and four-legged predators are extremely clever and nests will fail if you visit them and are watched doing so by unseen eyes. Make sure every nest in the garden is undisturbed. If you must peep inside do it in the warmth of mid-afternoon when the predators are least active.

Enigmatic bullfinch

There are over half a million pairs of bullfinches in Britain, concentrated mainly in the Midlands and south-east of England living in scrub, orchards, churchyards and gardens. The unfortunate bullfinch is the only one of our garden songbirds (if one excludes starling and house sparrow which can be legally controlled at any time) for which licences are regularly issued under the Wildlife and Countryside Act 1981 permitting them to be killed. Such licences are usually applied in the principal fruit growing areas eg Kent, Vale of Evesham.

The bullfinch's downfall lies in its habit of stripping the flower buds of apple, pear, cherry or other commercial fruit trees in spring. The birds know well that these are more nutritious than the leaf buds and they turn to them particularly in those years when their preferred foods of ash seed, dock and bramble are prematurely exhausted. If they attack your garden fruit trees use 'Transweb' (from Transatlantic Plastics Ltd., Ventnor, Isle of Wight) which is somewhat unsightly but effective. Should they launch into the gooseberry or currant bushes cover them temporarily with suspended strawberry netting.

The bullfinch is a secretive and enigmatic bird which has many habits unique to the rest of its

Although it is an attractive bird, the bullfinch can cause local damage to fruit trees; sometimes this damage can be serious at a commercial level.

47

family. Ian Newton in his wonderfully readable monograph on the finches (Collins, *New Naturalist* 1972) lists the oddities of the bullfinch's life which include the following:

> *Sexual behaviour which continues right through the year with hens always dominant over males.*
> *Nests solitarily: not territorial and not colonial.*
> *Completely inconspicuous in breeding season.*
> *No display flights; 'song' inaudible beyond yard or two from nest.*
> *Pair-formation involves ritual attack by hen on cock.*

Except when family parties are together for a few weeks at the end of the breeding season, bullfinches remain alone as a pair throughout the year; they do not forage in parties or flocks like most other finches, and appear totally oblivious to any other bullfinches that cross their path. They build an unusual two-layered twig nest in hedges and thickets and are only occasional visitors to the winter bird table. Although vegetarian for most of the year when they feed on seeds of chickweed, dandelion, dog's mercury, dock, birch and nettle among others, as well as their spring time weakness for fruit buds, they feed their young on protein rich caterpillars, spiders and small snails which they dexterously de-shell.

Help for house martins

Among the deluge of summer birds which decends on our gardens in April is the cheery house martin which arrives during the second half of the month. It has flown from West Africa, making a fast crossing of the Sahara at high level, unlike the more punishing low-level passage the swallows take wasting vital energy searching for non-existent insects en route. As soon as the house martins arrive last year's nests are inspected, most of them probably still intact and securely tucked up tight under the eaves. Necessary repairs are put in hand almost immediately. The house martin is one of the great mud-nest builders and cements its cup-shaped home firmly against the wall; with luck each nest will stay there for several years and need little repairing. One of the martin's many endearing traits is that it is fond of moving to new houses on suburban estates and will often colonise them almost before they are occupied by their human tenants. In years when April and May are very dry (are they ever nowadays?) the martins may be hard pressed to find mud so it is worth keeping watch for this and lending a hand by providing muddy puddles at their usual collection points if needed.

These are birds which will readily take to artifi-

The only time house martins willingly land on the ground is to collect mud for their plaster-work nests under the house eaves.

Before the end of March the first sand martins are back from a winter in Africa.

cial nests and if you want to attract them to your house it is well worth trying to do so. Although it is possible to fabricate perfectly good nests yourself out of Polyfilla or cement and sawdust if you are resourceful enough, it is much easier and not too expensive to buy them off the shelf. Nerine Nurseries, Welland, Malvern, Worcestershire WR13 6LN are good suppliers and the RSPB also sells them. The nests are easily fixed under eaves or below upstairs window sills and act as good starter homes to provide the foundation for a colony. They are most likely to be taken up if another colony already exists nearby. These artificial nests are fixed on hooks and can be easily lifted off to inspect contents. There is some evidence that they may be more successful on the north or east walls of buildings.

House sparrows not infrequently gatecrash the house martin nests either before the owners return from their winter in the sun or by ousting them once they have repaired the nests. To prevent this happening hang a series of weighted strings no more than 12 in (30 cm) in length and 6 in (15 cm) away from the entrance holes and at $2\frac{1}{2}$ in (6 cm) intervals. House martins approach the nests from below at a steep upward angle and will freely pass behind the strings which will easily and successfully deter the urchin sparrows with their level-flight approach.

Later in the season it is quite possible that a heavily loaded mud nest may break off the wall and spill the fledglings on the ground below. Get to them before the neighbour's cat and, using a ladder, replace them in a small open-top box, old blackbird nest or similar fixed to the wall close to the site they fell from, and there is every possibil-

ity that the parents will rear them successfully.

Some people take great exception to the accumulation of droppings below a house martin colony, especially if it is over a doorway or open window, but the problem can easily be solved by fixing a 9 in (22 cm) board some 6 ft (1.8 m) below the nests to trap the droppings. Either make the shelf removable on keyhole brackets, or use a ladder to clean it at the end of the season. Under the 1981 Wildlife and Countryside Act it is illegal to take, damage or destroy a house martin's nest while it is in use.

YOC Flight Line

Every year between the end of March and early May the Young Ornithologists' Club (YOC) runs a Phone-in on Tuesdays from 5.30pm to 7pm. Across the period of spring migration the public – both young and old – all over the country are encouraged to report their first sightings of all the summer migrants. The timings of the arrival of summer migrants varies from year to year and place to place depending on weather conditions in Europe and the prevailing wind directions and strength across the migration period. The success of the phone-in depends on the thousands of people who report their sightings; in an average year over 5,000 reports are filed in. Records will vary from early wheatears and sand martins, to passing ospreys, the first cuckoos, a dozen different warblers, rare bee-eater or hoopoe and then, in May, the last arrivals of all – swift, hobby, nightjar and spotted flycatcher. In this way maps are drawn up each year to chart the spread of arrival of all these spring birds. So when you see summer

The hobby is a late spring arrival, often recorded by the YOC Flight Line.

migrants arriving, telephone one of the Flight-Line numbers – you will be answered by a volunteer who will want to know:

1 Species seen
2 When and where you saw your migrant
3 How many you saw
4 How you identified the migrant

The volunteer will also be able to tell you about other migrants seen in your county.

Look out for up-to-date information on the Flight Line on Ceefax **295**. Flight Line telephone numbers are:

Sandy	**0767 80551**
Shoreham-by-Sea	**0273 463642**
Norwich	**0603 615920**
Exeter	**0392 32691**
Lincoln	**0522 35596**
Huddersfield	**0484 356331 or 517588**
Newcastle-on-Tyne	**091 23 24148**
Newtown (Powys)	**0686 27219**
Edinburgh	**031 556 5624 or 556 9042**
Belfast	**0232 692547**
Dublin	**875759**

A summary of the results of Flight Line is available from 1st August by sending two first class stamps to YOC, The Lodge, Sandy, Bedfordshire SG19 2DL.

Building supplies for nests

Birds use a wide range of materials to build their nests. Jackdaws will stuff the chimney with a cartload of sticks, and line the nest with wool and grasses; smaller birds use grasses, hairs, moss and feathers. The long-tailed tit and goldcrest, architects of the most delicate nests of all, weave their tiny masterpieces of spiders web, filaments of lichen and moss, and tiny feathers. Birds are very willing to be helped with supplies for their building work so do not hesitate to put out suitable materials in mesh bags for them to help themselves. Hang one bag up from a tree and peg another to the ground to accommodate all tastes. Use more or less what you can find available, perhaps avoiding bright colours as these tend to make the nests a bit conspicuous. Clean straw, surplus hay, sheeps wool, dry moss, dog and cat combings are all welcome. Or you can add short lengths of cotton or wool, horsehair or the small feathers from spent cushions. You will find that much of the material is taken with gusto. Birds are sensible enough to take advantage of a ready-made builder's yard if they are given the chance rather than spend time searching. Providing a central supply depot like this will also help you to locate where the various pairs are nesting as it is relatively easy to watch them back to the nest with their bundles of soft bedding. It also has the additional advantage of removing the need for you to 'beat about the bush' looking for nests and risk exposing them to predators.

Mirrors and reflections

The one thing above all others which is like a red rag to a bull for the highly charged, territory-owning male bird in spring is the sight or sound of another male in his back yard. A frequent technique used nowadays by those researching different aspects of bird behaviour is to play back a tape recording of its own song so that it is irresistably lured into the open to confront and repel the 'intruder'. Similarly the sight of an intruder will throw robin, chaffinch or pied wagtail into paroxysms of rage even if in reality it is only a mirrored reflection of its own aggression.

Two officers of the Sussex constabulary drove their car into a layby at Hastings for a breather (unmarked patrol car; Triumph Dolomite; colour post-office red; black vinyl roof). They were immediately confronted by a pied wagtail (no disguise; coloured black and white; demeanour aggressive). The bird landed on the bonnet and walked menacingly towards the wing-mirror, inspected the image it saw and launched itself into a measured assault on it. The only respite it had over the next few minutes was the walk back and forth across the bonnet to the other mirror where he found yet another combatant awaiting him. Slowly recovering their composure the patrol men drove off in order to try to relieve the situation until the wagtail slid off the bonnet as the car reached 20 mph and then, – carefully observing the speed limit – hotly pursued the car, as close to the wing mirror as it could get, until the car's speed outdid it and it left, presumably elated at the success in driving off both intruders so fast and so far.

Pied wagtails have been recorded attacking their mirror images more times than any other species but many other birds will do the same. House windows often act as good mirrors from the outside and birds quite frequently assault their own reflections in them. A carrion crow launched into its reflection in a bedroom window in mid-Wales at 4.30 each morning for several weeks until the infuriated occupant lay in wait and despatched it to eternity. Magpies, chaffinches and blackbirds will do the same and bullfinch and blackcap have both been recorded actually killing themselves as a result of their frenetic battles. Dippers quite frequently attack their window images in the early mornings and we were recently able to watch one – urged on by the admiring hen – from inside the window of a mill house in South Devon at a range of no more than three feet.

Nest-building materials supplied on the lawn.

A male wagtail launches itself at its own mirror-reflection.

It is rather strange that birds can be duped so easily. They show considerable refinement in their ability to recognise visual images and one would think they would quickly recognise the reflections for what they are. If you should have a window at which a male bird is belabouring an imagined rival, spare him the pain and trouble by putting a sheet of pale paper – a newsheet will do – on the inside and this will probably destroy the reflection.

Collared doves

As recently as the mid-1950's collared doves were unknown in Britain but twenty years later, at the end of a great rush of westwards expansion across Europe from their original home in India, collared doves had colonised all the suitable areas of Britain and are now one of our familiar town-and-country birds. They have a close relationship with man and are commonest in suburbs, small towns and villages and around farms. They are grain eaters and rely especially on ready access to spilled corn at grain stores, cereal farms, warehouses and wharfs. As a result of which they are now one of only thirteen British birds which are on the schedule of bird species which can be legally controlled at any time under the Wildlife and Countryside Act. In only twenty years they graduated from first appearance to being listed as an official pest. Around towns and villages they will share grain in chicken runs and farm yards but also feed on berries and young foliage. Important for the bird gardener is the fact that they also come readily to garden feeding stations for peas, seeds, grain and a miscellany of scraps. They are regular visitors in many bird gardens and from April through to autumn their three-note cooing, *coo, coo, coo,* (a strong emphasis on the second note) is a soft and gentle sound of summer, although there are those who regard its constant repetition as painfully monotonous. If it sings regularly around your garden you can guarantee it is nesting on its flimsy platform of twigs somewhere nearby, probably in conifers if they occur, and through the summer this successful invader will produce successive broods of young, two at a time as is the case with all pigeons and doves.

Blue tits at the nest box

Provide a nest box for blue tits or great tits and one or other is almost certain to take up the offer. Blue tits are nearly twice as numerous as their larger cousins and are very easy to tempt into boxes (see page 103). There are already a lot of suitable natural holes in the buildings, trees or walls of a good garden but these will readily be ignored in favour of your made-to-measure blue tit prefab. The male blue tit will be the first to inspect the potential home. He will perch at the entrance, look in a few times and if he likes what he sees will slowly turn his head from side to side to

Once they have left the nest, young birds are in the most vulnerable period of their lives. Many will succumb at this time.

53

The collared dove is the most successful of recent bird colonists in Britain being common now in nearly all areas.

show his smart white cheeks to the female by way of invitation and perhaps peck gently at the sides of the hole. Nest selection is a serious business however and she will not be rushed, especially as there are probably alternative properties to inspect as well. Once they begin to settle for your nest box the male will then enter the box as a further enticement and it may still be a couple of weeks before the hen goes in, but once she does you can be fairly sure they will stay.

When the time is right both birds will set about building the nest, bringing in first a base of fine twigs, strips of inner bark and grass, shortly followed by beakfuls of moss to form the foundation of the nest. As the nest takes shape the hen forms the deep cup by wriggling and turning round in it while she continues to build up the sides. Unlike other tits they will line the furnished cup with a cosy layer of small feathers.

It is not always so easy however and prime nest sites have to be fought for. The blue tit is a pugnacious customer and can hold his own reasonably well against most competitors. Great tit and nut-hatch are the two bigger and stronger adversaries against which the blue tit is normally outweighed, but even then disputes can last several days with alternating occupations before the outcome is finally settled. If the blue tit was well established first it is quite possible that his persistent resolve will eventually deter even the aggression of nut-hatch or great tit. Birds such as marsh tit, coal tit, and treecreeper are much more easily ejected by blue tits.

Egg laying in the blue tit nest happens around the last week of April. The hen bird, who will lay between nine and twelve eggs at the rate of one per day, has to be in prime condition for the combined weight of these eggs formed in her body and laid across a period of twelve days will be some one and a half times her own body weight. If you peep in the nest box during the laying period (incubation does not start until the last egg has been laid) do not be alarmed if you see no eggs because, in order to hide them while she is away the hen will carefully cover them each time by pulling part of the nest lining over them.

MAY

The parent blue tits make endless visits to the nest box to satisfy their youngsters' appetites.

Feeding the family

Around the middle of May, at the end of fourteen days of continuous incubation the blue tit eggs will hatch in their nest box home. From now on it is all-action as both parents seek to satisfy the insatiable appetites of ten tiny tits. Initially the demands are not too great but as the days pass and the baby nestlings grow, their appetites increase too. In the first day or two the adults make perhaps 400 daily nest visits between them; ten days later when the fledglings are nearly ready to leave the nest the visits have increased to about 700 per day! Now the crucial importance of the territory, fought for so hard in early spring, can be seen. The parent birds forage without pause, enjoying the feeding site which is their own and without the hassle involved in disputing ownership with neighbours. The breeding season has been timed so that the baby blue tits are growing at exactly the time when the huge caterpillar crop on oak leaves and the little spider cocoons among the new shoots are at their most plentiful. Foremost of the foods for blue tits at this season – and for many of the other woodland birds – are the caterpillars and pupae of the tiny oak roller moth (*Tortrix viridana*) and the winter moth (*Operophtera brumata*). The blue tits collect the swarming caterpillars from the oak tree leaves and are quick and expert at extracting the pupae from inside the rolled up leaves. During this non-stop caterpillar food-shuttle the adults must feed themselves too but as part of their time and motion strategy they eat only the smallest caterpillars themselves. By doing this they avoid making wasteful trips back to the nest with light-weight loads, but only ferry the biggest and most succulent. Just as long as the youngsters in the box shout for food the adults keep bringing it; that is the stimulus to which they respond and only if the young are sated and sleeping will the feeding rate drop and the tired parents have time to rest, feed and preen.

Now the nest box is full of heaving, wriggling youngsters try to restrain yourself from looking in too often. Keep your visits down to one every two or three days and choose a moment when you know the parents are away. As fledging time approaches be extra careful for an ill-timed visit may result in the young 'exploding' from the box before they can fly properly. If this should happen collect them together and pop them gently back through the hole, covering it then for a minute or two while they settle and then very slowly removing the cover.

Despite the large number of mouths to feed the nesting success of tit families is high and in many years the number which die in the nest is less than five per cent. The bigger the brood, the greater the number of mouths that have to be fed from the same amount of food which the parents can bring and it has been shown that young tits fledging from smaller broods are fitter and heavier when they leave the nest, and survive better in the following winter than the young from big broods. So whereas all the titmice lay large clutches of eggs and follow a policy of 'safety in numbers' it seems that the strategy is perhaps being pushed to the limit a bit. Once the family leaves the relative safety of the nest box the losses will begin. This is the next time of great danger for the youngsters and a time when the garden predators will find easy prey.

Unfledged tawny owls

The tawny owl, the wise old owl of nursery stories and folk tales, is the bird lodger which remains unseen in most gardens. This night owl is not only a denizen of rural woodlands but is a plentiful town dweller as well and a successful hunter in

urban and suburban gardens and parks. During the day it is out of sight roosting in the leafy depths of an ivy-covered tree or tall holly. Tawny owls are early nesters, choosing a site in a deep tree hole, old magpie's nest or specially constructed nest box and laying eggs well before the end of March. By early May the young owlets are two or three weeks old. Although they still have another three weeks to go before they will be able to fly the mother tawny owl now calls them out from the nest hole. The owlets emerge to climb gamely onto the branches of the tree scrabbling about with bill, feet and rudimentary wings. It is a tall order and many fail to make it safely on to the big branches and fall to the soft ground below. At this time of year innumerable 'abandoned owlets' are reported to the RSPB and other organisations but the advice has to be, 'Put them back where you found them'. During the daytime they will crouch in the leaf litter or the rank grass beneath the nest tree and in the gathering twilight call for food. The parents will find them without fail and feed them until they are strong-winged and fledged.

It is interesting to see how ferociously and effectively these mini-owls can defend themselves, throwing themselves onto their backs, opening and snapping their bills threateningly and presenting a spiked umbrella of flashing talons. One thing you may be able to do if the tree lends itself to it, is to place the grounded youngster in a crotch or on a level area on one of the biggest low branches, preferably close to the trunk. It is a safe bet that its siblings are tucked away in similar spots nearby. Beware of the female owl however because she can be very aggressive and genuinely dangerous in defence of the nest or the young and will not shun from 'bombing' you as you inspect the owlet; you could be raked by her talons and there have been some nasty injuries to people looking into tawny owl nests. So if you have a pair in your owl-box and are tempted to investigate there is only one really safe piece of advice: don't.

Meat and no veg

With the limitless abundance of free insect meat available in May and June even the most dedicated of vegetarian seed-eaters allow their normal principles to slip to take advantage of the meat feast. Insect food is much more nutritious for growing chicks and therefore many of the garden birds will change diets on that account. An inveterate seed-eater such as the greenfinch, for example, will bring a mixture of seeds and caterpillars to the youngsters. During the first few days of

Young tawny owls leave their cramped nest hole well before they can fly and sit among the branches where they are fed by the parents at night.

their lives insects comprise almost all their food and seeds are only gradually increased; slowly the balance is tipped and by the time they leave the nest they are proper seed-eating finches. Goldfinches and bullfinches adopt a similar pattern but the bullfinch has a particular problem with insect collecting because the bull-nosed shape of its bill does not lend itself easily to the task; it collects caterpillars, spiders and — improbably — small snails which it deftly deshells to feed to the nestlings. The chaffinch completely forswears its seed diet for the period when young are being reared and resorts to the universal small caterpillars supplemented with a variety of spiders, leaf-eating bugs, earwigs, beetles and even small moths and flies caught on the wing.

Even the shy hawfinch takes advantage of the crop of winter moth and oak roller caterpillars in May, temporarily abandoning its fruit and seed diet. The hawfinch is a rather strange and secretive bird, a real bonus for you in the garden if you are fortunate enough to have them. They are commonest in the south and east and have a special fondness for the dwindling areas of cherry orchards which provide them with a good supply of cherry kernels. The bird's massive head, large bill and enormous jaw muscles, which give it the pouch-cheeked look, enable it to open seeds as hard as cherry stones and sloes, although much of the usual food is made up of softer seeds such as elm, hornbeam and hawthorn. This great bill is a complex structure acting like a skilfully designed vice which allows a bird weighing only 2 oz (55 g) to crack a cherry stone by exerting a force calculated at 60–90 pounds! Hawfinches can deal with olive stones too (they require a force of nearer 150 pounds) so if you have hawfinches in the area think about keeping your summer cherry stones and your party olive stones and trying to lure them down onto the ground in autumn or winter.

The tiny oak-leaf caterpillars are food for all at this time of year and they are present in uncountable thousands on each oak. In years of heaviest infestation they will completely defoliate some trees which will then have to produce another leaf crop, usually referred to as the Lammas growth. Jackdaws, which are normally grassland feeders with a diet of over eighty per cent of vegetable food will take advantage of such plagues and for a week or two in May can be seen in flocks incongruously balancing on the flimsy twigs in the tops of the oak trees.

Four-footed predators

Most birds will die when they are young, during the first nine months of their lives, but once they have passed the twelve-month mark their chances of living to old age are quite good. Many people are understandably upset by the thought – or the sight – of predators taking garden birds but on the one hand the predators presumably have as much right to exist as the prey and on the other hand it is quite unrealistic for us to pretend that we can completely protect our garden birds from predators all the time. Let us console ourselves with the knowledge that the predator-prey relationship is basically a healthy one and has advantages to both parties, not just to the predator. Nonetheless it is valuable to know the predators and not do anything in the garden which will unfairly expose birds to unnecessary risks.

Cats . . .

The number one enemy of garden birds without question is the domestic cat. Cats are by nature hunters and it is not their fault if they come into frequent conflict with the bird gardener. In Britain now there are literally millions of cats and it is a lucky garden which is completely free of them. Cats are a particular hazard in the nesting season and take a heavy toll of youngsters which have just left the nest. Adult birds too are at high risk when nesting because they are obliged to live at the nest throughout that time and cats can very quickly learn where these are located. Thick,

The domestic cat is the most serious of all garden predators and can take a heavy toll on small birds.

59

The introduced grey squirrel is a resourceful and persistent predator in some gardens.

thorny hedges of holly, hawthorn and blackthorn will make it more difficult for them to reach the nests. Try to make sure that nest boxes are well out of reach so that arriving and departing parents are not put at risk, but also so that the presence of a cat sitting underneath or on a neighbouring branch does not inhibit the parents from feeding the young. If there is persistent interference the adults may decide to cut their losses and desert the nest. Some cats, particularly Siamese, are adept at catching birds (and bats) on the wing by leaping high in the air as they skim over and this should be borne in mind in relation to surrounding cover when locating bird-baths etc.

In the simplest terms birds and cats are incompatible in the same garden and the ideal would be to exclude cats completely if possible. This is not usually feasible however and other precautions and deterrants need to be employed.

The first precaution should be to make it difficult for cats to approach the places where birds are feeding or nesting. Their main hunting strategies are either to stalk, or to lie in wait, both of which require good ground cover. So make sure that all nest boxes are erected where it is not easy for cats to hide nearby and that bird tables and other feeding devices, including ground feeding sites are well out in the open. It may seem strange to suggest having a cat of your own but this does have some points to commend it, because cats are essentially territorial and will act as a deterrent to too much invasion by neighbours. A tom is a better choice than a queen because he is fairly lazy and less likely to develop into a bird hunter than the female; she will also attract all the local admirers when she is in season. So the best option if you are going to have a cat is to settle for a well-fed, neutered tom who will act as a lazy stay-at-home

By the first days of May screaming parties of swifts have returned to enliven the skies over most of our towns and villages.

deterrent to at least some of the other local cats. Whatever you choose consider the merits of fitting your cat with a collar and bell from an early age so that the birds always know when it is around. Your problems will also be eased if the cat can be kept indoors during as many of the daylight hours as possible, especially the early morning and before dusk when bird feeding is at its greatest intensity.

If you are catless however and you cannot effectively fence neighbouring cats out, resort to other deterrents. Cats will soon realise where they are not welcome and a concentrated campaign of shouting, chasing and waving will help them get the message. Back it up if necessary with a bombardment of water bags, well directed hose pipe or other 'soft' missiles as they run away and they will be reluctant to spend much time in your garden. There are proprietory deterrents on the market but they become expensive because they have to be put down repeatedly and probably do not make much sense in most gardens. A good catting dog can work wonders and very quickly persuade the local cat population that your garden is not a good place to be. An enthusiastic dog alas may also do a fairly good demolition job on the garden beds in his zeal for pursuit.

... and other four-legged enemies

Weasels are the most regular and potentially the most destructive of wild mammal predators in the bird garden. They are skilled birds' nesters and they can be a special problem with nest boxes once they discover that such nests annually contain a ready made meal neatly presented. They will then search them out and go through a series of nest boxes systematically. They are excellent climbers and their long thin bodies can easily pass through the $1\frac{1}{8}$ in (2.8 cm) holes which are the recommended size for small hole-nesting birds. Another mammal which is a considerable egg thief given half a chance is the wood mouse (long-tailed field mouse). It too can climb like a steeplejack and will quickly learn the advantages of visiting nest boxes. In some years of plague they run riot through woodland nest boxes and unfortunately may deal similarly with any garden boxes which are fixed to trees before you even know you have them there. Weasel and wood mouse predation is therefore difficult to avoid. One system which certainly works although it looks a bit unsightly (it also prevents squirrel and cat exploration) is the fitting of cylinders or cones $\frac{3}{4}$ in or 1 in (2 or 2.5 cm) wire netting mesh around the entrance

61

The more varied the habitats in the garden, the wider will be the range of species using it.

holes. Fix the netting firmly but loosely to the box so that it is unstable and gives no purchase for climbing animals and make it about 4 in (10 cm) in diameter and about 6 in or 7 in (15 or 18 cm) in depth. It is possible to obtain mouse repellant (Sutton's seed merchants) in pellet form which has been shown to be effective when used around nest box trees.

Dormice may seem unlikely nest predators but they will occasionally take over a nest box which is in use. We know of garden pied flycatcher nests in which a dormouse has entered the box, eaten the eggs and then curled up in the nest and gone to sleep. Even lifting him out for the family to inspect didn't wake him up! Dormice are scarce and attractive small creatures and you may well feel privileged if they do decide to patronise your garden, even if it is to the detriment of an occasional nest.

The final two mammals have very little to commend them. Rats must always be regarded as a serious pest and early steps taken to eliminate them. As a householder and ratepayer you should turn first to your local environmental health department and seek their help. Many local authorities have their own rat catcher (the Ministry of Agriculture no longer does) and they have a duty to investigate if you report to them that you have rats around your house or in the adjoining buildings. If your problem is restricted to the garden it may be more difficult to persuade them to come out. Should you decide to deal with the rats yourself the best way is with a 'safe' rat poison. Place the baited food in a length of drainpipe or similar device well out of reach of domestic animals or birds. 'Raticate' or 'Warfarin' are two of the safest rat baits currently on the market. Traps are the other method of trying to control these undesirable animals but they are extremely suspicious and especially wary of the conventional break-back type; wire 'live traps' may work better, baited with cheese, kitchen scraps or stale cake. Be extremely careful about siting traps however to ensure that you do not catch cats, birds or other non-target creatures. Preferably use them in a locked shed where you know rats will go.

Grey squirrels were introduced into Britain from North America in the latter half of last century and apart from the fact that they look attractive (but barely even that compared to our disappearing native red squirrel) and are accomplished acrobats, they have precious little to commend them. Their worst crime is the serious damage they cause to young hardwood trees but they are also accomplished egg thieves. As well as taking eggs or young from open nests of blackbird, collared dove or greenfinch, they will also raid nest boxes, even widening the entrance if necessary to get at the family within. Take a hard line with grey squirrels: shoot or trap them if you can because they are no good to man nor beast in the bird garden or anywhere else.

May arrivals and some exotics

As May comes in there are still one or two of the latest summer arrivals to put in their first appearance. In the first days of the month swifts are at last arcing and screaming across the sky high above the houses. They delay their arrival until now to ensure that the aerial supply of tiny midges and flies is sufficient to sustain them and help bring them rapidly in to breeding condition once they are here. Their stay with us will be the shortest of any of the summer birds and in fourteen brief weeks or so the skies will once again be empty of these high speed daredevil fliers.

The spotted flycatcher is another late arrival in May because it too is in no hurry to get under way with nesting, being dependent for its food on the larger flying insects which are at their peak in June, July and August. It is more sensible for the flycatcher to extend its season with second broods into late summer when the harvest is still good rather than begin too early and risk the young going short of food. The spotted flycatcher's rather plain plumage is compensated by its confiding nature,

The rare and colourful hoopoe occasionally turns up unexpectedly in May or June: an exotic wanderer from Mediterranean countries.

The delicate pied flycatcher (female illustrated) is a common bird in rural gardens in western Britain and takes very readily to nest boxes.

fine upright stance and striking behaviour. Sitting on a prominent perch or the lower branches of a big tree it darts out into the sunlight to snap up a passing insect, hovering or twisting agilely and then dashing back to the perch. It eats large prey such as horseflies and butterflies and can readily tell the difference between wasps, bees and the harmless hoverflies and beeflies which mimic them for protection. They will carefully remove the stings from wasps or bees before eating them. The best possible way to help spotted flycatchers in the garden is by ensuring that you have a wealth of insect-attracting flowers to provide the host of butterflies, moths, bees and hoverflies which they need. Provide a nest site or two for them as well, in the creeper on the house wall or under the porch roof.

May is also the time to start listening for the soft purring call of turtle doves. These are commonest in southern England and sadly very scarce in the north and west. At least fifty per cent of the turtle dove's diet is made up of the seeds of fumi-tory, a common but declining weed of cultivated ground and waste places, but turtle doves also feed on seeds of plantain, chickweed and other weeds. If there are allotments or disused gravel workings near you they may well be the sort of areas that attract this beautiful dove. Fumitory does not produce its first seed until May and therefore the turtle dove's arrival must be timed to coincide with it. The distribution of fumitory and turtle doves in Britain, not surprisingly, shows a very close relationship. Most pairs of these doves will rear two broods, but in August they are likely to abandon the nest whatever stage of eggs or young it contains, in order to build up their own resources and moult new feathers preparatory to an abrupt departure to Africa in early September.

May is prime-time viewing for any real exotics that may turn up in the garden as overshooting migrants from their normal breeding areas in France or elsewhere on the Continent. The hoopoe is the most likely, more so in the south of England than elsewhere, and every year there are a

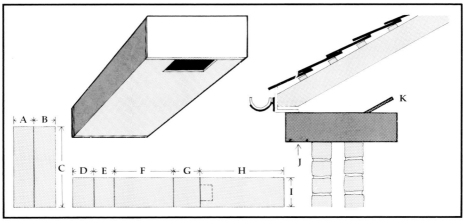

Construction details for a swift nest box.

KEY

A Side 5¼ in (14 cm)	**D** Front 5½ in (14 cm)	**H** Floor with hole 20 in (50 cm)
B Side 5½ in (14 cm)	**E** Back 5½ in (14 cm)	**I** Width 8 in (20 cm)
C Side 20 in (50 cm)	**F** Roof 14 in (35 cm)	**J** Entrance
	G Door 6 in (15 cm)	**K** Inspection lid

number of reports of surprised householders looking out to find a hoopoe feeding on the lawn. Just occasionally these wanderers may succeed in finding a mate and staying to nest if they are tempted by warm dry weather at the right time. They will look for a good cavity in an old wall or stockdove sized hole in a big apple tree, but don't start laying plans for it because it won't happen to more than the lucky one or two.

A pied flycatcher's home in the west

If you are fortunate enough to have your garden in rural Wales, the English borders, Lake District or parts of northern England, north Devon or Somerset there is one particularly fine summer bird which is even easier to attract into a nest box than blue tits are in other parts of the country. This nest-box bird *par excellence* is the pied flycatcher; if you have oak trees nearby put a nest box up in your garden in these areas and you are almost guaranteed to have a pair there in the first year. They are really oak woodland birds – yet another species that feasts on the innumerable hoards of little green oak leaf caterpillars – but they are not all that fussy and will happily settle where a good insect crop can be found on hawthorn, willow, alder, birch or a mixture of other native trees. If anything they are even more confiding than spotted flycatchers and will nest very close to the house. Without doubt these are one of the most attractive of all our summer visitors. The male's

bold pied plumage is conspicuous and on his forehead are two little spots which he sports like a diminutive pair of white pince-nez spectacles. The female's pattern is similar but skewbald instead of pied and she lacks the spectacles. Pied flycatchers arrive towards the end of April, after blue tits and other resident hole-nesters have claimed their nest sites. A useful trick to ensure that a nest box is kept free for the flycatchers is to close the entrance until the male has arrived and is singing. They often sing very close to the box, even sitting on top of it, so you have an easy cue for removing the closure.

Garden mimics

The roof-top starling is hardly one of our more accomplished singers but what he may lack in style and melody he certainly makes up in panache and enthusiasm. His basic repertoire consists of a rambling improvisation of husky warblings, clickings and musical whistlings strung loosely together. However, in among these will be thrown an almost baffling array of other sounds, for the starling is far and away the most accomplished mimic among our garden birds (the rare marsh warbler has an even bigger range). The starling will borrow song phrases and calls from a wide range of other birds; examples are almost irrelevant because, depending on where you and your starlings live, it may include buzzard, chaffinch, swallow, redshank, greylag or partridge. You name it and the starling will copy it. Its skill is

Starlings are the most accomplished mimics amongst all our British birds.

not limited to wild sounds and it will happily incorporate a telephone bell, factory whistle, lawnmower or the neighbourhood cat. Why does the starling bother to broaden its repertoire in such an amazing way? The answer remains a bit of an enigma but it is suggested that as a starling goes on learning additional sounds to build into its song he becomes more appealing to the females on the basis that 'Gosh, he's got a huge repertoire, he must be an old bird and therefore an experienced mate'. By the same token he may well appear a more daunting prospect to other male pretenders.

The starling is not the only practiced mimic in the garden. The skylark, singing high overhead, is renowned for his powers although they do not rival those of the starling. Neither indeed are they as impressive as the imitations that can be produced by a blackcap. A coloratura in its own right the blackcap can include rich phrases from other fine singers too. At least sixteen different species have been recorded including nightingale (frequent), blackbird, willow warbler, song thrush and redstart. Blackcap and garden warbler songs are notoriously difficult to tell apart at the best of times; the fact that a blackcap freely mimics the

song of garden warblers will provide the ultimate test for the garden birdwatcher who claims infallibility in separating the two by song.

Another unlikely garden mimic is the jay whose harsh raucous call seems far removed from a polished skill in artistry. But we should never underestimate the skill of any member of the crow family and the jay can produce extremely good imitations of birds such as buzzard, heron, tawny owl, pheasant and lapwing. Such calls are not strung together as part of any attempted song – even the jay itself would surely never pretend to possessing a song – but are offered in isolation, improbable calls of a heron from a rhododendron bush or lapwing from a conifer plantation.

Nest box for swifts

Swifts nest in colonies in roof spaces of houses, churches or other buildings where they can find easy access through the open eaves which characterise many older structures. Most buildings that are put up nowadays have closed eaves and are no use to swifts and in fact the species is scarcer now than it used to be in many towns and cities simply because all the old buildings have been replaced by unsuitable modern ones. Swifts will however use special nest boxes erected under the eaves and they can be made and fitted in the following way.

Using $\frac{3}{4}$ in (1.8 cm) thick timber, make a closed box 20 in (50 cm) long × 8 in (20 cm) × $5\frac{1}{2}$ in (14 cm). Leave an entrance hole at one end of the intended floor of the box and on the opposite side at the far end make a simple hinged lid (use webbing or a strip of rubber for the hinge if you wish, as it will be inside the roof of the building and does not need to be weatherproof). This will enable you to inspect the box from inside when it is installed, and to clean it out. Erect the box either by removing one of the bricks from under the eaves of the roof or whatever other similar step may be necessary. Instal the box so that the entrance hole is facing the ground beneath and is set back almost level with the outside edge of the wall. Encourage use of the box by putting a twisted ring of straw at the far end of the nest box and block the entrance until the swifts have arrived if you want to make sure the sparrows do not take it over. The box should be at least 12–14 ft above the ground and beyond that can be as high up as you like. Remember that swifts enter the nests with a deep upward swoop from below so ensure there is no neighbouring wall or roof too close to prevent a straight run in.

JUNE

S pring is not what it used to be' we tell ourselves and certainly in recent years we seem to wait endlessly for the warmth and sunshine through April and May only to find the lingering damp and cold of winter passing straight into early summer. Enjoy the abundant bird activity in the garden as fully as you can in the warm and golden days in May and the early heat of flaming June because it lasts so short a time. All too soon the freshness of leaves darkens, the best intensity of bird song diminishes and the bustle of spring becomes lost in the sultry quiet of high summer. For the time being these are the weeks of reward for all the hard work that has gone into the bird garden through the year; a time when enjoying the flush of springtime is the pay off for time and money spent in fostering the garden sanctuary.

Even as early as mid-June signs of the passing breeding season are apparent. Almost before we have really begun to appreciate the nesting activity all around us the first flocks of young starlings are on the lawn. Starlings are normally single brooded, and with youngsters now out of the nest their season is nearly over. In the riverside meadows lapwings are gathering in flocks which will remain together right through until March next year. Improbable though it may seem some of these birds already comprise small groups which have migrated here from the lowlands of western Europe.

By the second half of the month the dawn chorus is noticeably less intense than it was earlier and throughout the day the volume of song is clearly diminishing. Pairs of birds such as tawny owls and blue tits, both of which normally rear only one brood, have seen their young out of the nest and except for the contact calls and the food-begging cries of the young, they too are silent now as the adults no longer need to sing to proclaim their rights to territory. Others which still have bursting nests full of hungry babies must spend the entire time fetching and carrying food and do not have the time to sing; now they must rely on the work they did earlier in the season in agreeing their territorial boundaries with their neighbours.

'Abandoned' fledglings

A grating and insistent chirping from the back of the flower border is an easy give-away to the presence of a newly fledged song thrush crouching fat-bellied, stump-tailed and guileless on the ground among the plants at the base of the hedge.

Brothers and sisters are doubtless close by but with luck they are sensibly perched in the depths of the thick prickly hedge where they will be a little safer than the wide-eyed innocent sitting on the ground. For the first day or two after they have left the nest the fledglings ability to fly will be rudimentary; they may be quite good at flying downwards but pretty hopeless going back up. During this time they are in the most vulnerable period of their lives, unable to defend themselves, unequipped for escape and soft targets for a garden predator. This is the time of year above all others to keep the cat indoors during the daytime! The parent birds will continue to feed the youngsters when they are out of the nest for a week or two (double-brooded pairs may even have to feed two consecutive broods of young at the same time) and during the early days of the period after they leave the nest the youngsters readily give the impression of being lost and forsaken. But they are not really abandoned, so harden your heart a little and resist the obvious temptation to take them in and look after them yourself. Watch carefully and you will see that the parents do know where they are and are bringing food to them regularly. It may indeed be a dangerous and vulnerable time for these hopefuls but it is a gauntlet they have to run and we should leave them to take their chance, knowing that the parents will bring them the food they need. It is a much better option than taking their fate into our own hands.

Grounded swifts

The swift is the most aerial of all our birds (see page 77) with wings designed for fast and sustained flight. From tip to tip their wings are nearly 20 in (50 cm) across compared to a body length of only $6\frac{1}{2}$ in (16.5 cm) and although they are perfectly designed for rapid streamlined flight and aerial manoeuvres these wings can land the swift in trouble should it accidentally be forced onto the ground. It is infrequent for swifts to end up in such trouble, perhaps because they have made a careless exit from the nest or have collided with a neighbour outside the nest hole. Once they are on the ground they are usually marooned. The legs are so short and weak that they cannot be used to give the bird the thrust it needs for a vertical lift-off in the way other birds do and the wings are so long that they cannot give a downbeat below body level. If you find a grounded swift handle it carefully and avoid any possible damage to the wings by keeping them closed to its body. Swifts are completely incapable of harming you

If a swift becomes accidentally grounded its long wings make it impossible for it to take off again unaided.

(although we know of at least one instance when two policemen, summoned to help, refused to touch the bird or allow anyone else to without the local birdwatcher being summoned, because they believed it was a 'fierce and dangerous bird of prey'). Take the chance of examining it while you have it; feel the stiff, strong flight feathers and the needle-sharp claws (it so seldom lands anywhere that they never have the chance to get worn down or blunted) and do not be too alarmed if a few little flat flies run over the feathers or come onto your arm. These somewhat obnoxious blood-sucking creatures are louse flies, *Crataerina pallida*, which are the swift's worst enemy and permanent lodgers in the nests, awaiting the birds' return each year; they are not interested in human blood however and will quickly reject you.

To return your stranded swift to the air carry it to a wide open space and launch it by throwing it firmly upwards 10 ft or 12 ft (3–4 m) and it will fly off happily, shake its feathers into shape and join the rest of the wheeling colony in the sky above.

Weeds for wildlife

By mid-summer the hedge bottoms, the orchard and farthest corners of the garden become rank and overgrown with nettles, brambles, thistles, docks and other invasive weeds. The time is right for the tidy-minded gardener to get out his strimmer or scrub cutter and cut back these patches before they take over the garden or cast unwelcome seeds over the neighbour's hedge. However, hold on! It may be even more important to consider the role of some of these familiar weeds in the wider web of garden wildlife. Earlier in the book we have seen that gardens in Britain occupy upwards of 700,000 acres and at a time when wild areas in the countryside have never been scarcer and farm fields are 'cleaned' of most of their wild weeds, our gardens, orchards and allotments become more and more important as refuges for many of these native field weeds. Lots of familiar and popular species of garden wildlife – insects and mammals as well as birds – depend upon these native plants; for example we have seen how turtle doves occur only in those parts of the country where fumitory is present. Remember too that in the garden Master Plan we identified the retention of rough corners as one of the prime aims of any complete bird garden. Birds which are seed eaters are noticeably reluctant to take advantage of many of the seeds of introduced garden flowers in the way that berry-eaters have capitalised on non-native berry-bearing plants. A home-grown crop of native weeds is indispensible and will encour-

The whitethroat is one of the birds which feeds readily on berries of black bryony – poisonous to humans.

age butterflies, moths, hoverflies, and a host of other insects during the flowering season, and birds to feed on the seeds or berries in autumn and winter. Your tolerance in allowing them will be rewarded by an increased range of wildlife using the garden. The caterpillars of small tortoiseshell butterflies for example will only feed on the fresh leaves of stinging nettles; there are many similar examples.

In summer and autumn the numbers of goldfinches, chaffinches and linnets which come to feed on the garden seed heads will be counted in twos and threes. Do not expect them in flocks, because it won't actually happen that way. The big flocks demand wide open fields where they can rely on an enormous volume of weed seeds lying in the soil; the nearest you may get to large numbers is by letting your allotment run away with itself a little in late summer, especially if one or two other gardeners have done the same.

In the following tables we list some of the main 'weed' species which are important to birds. Many of them are much used by other forms of wildlife as well. There are many bird gardeners throughout the country who spurn order and cultivation and actively encourage the development of a truly wild garden for the benefits it brings for wildlife – and there is probably an equal number who do it by default! This is their choice, but we believe that there is actually more that can be achieved for birds and others through the sort of planned approach which we suggest. Within this plan it is up to you how much of a wild patch you can afford to leave: only one plea, make it as big as you can – a pocket-handkerchief size won't get you very far, but even that is better than nothing.

Spotted flycatchers are confiding birds which will often nest on or near houses, unconcerned about human proximity.

Vegetable patch weeds

Dandelion (*Taraxicum officinale*)	Bullfinch, goldfinch, greenfinch, redpoll, siskin
Plantains (*Plantago spp*)	Linnet
Annual meadow grass (Poa annua)	Linnet, goldfinch
Forget-me-nots (*Myosotis spp*)	Linnet, tree sparrow
Betony (*Betonica officinalis*)	Goldfinch
Chickweed (*Stellaria & Cerastium spp*)	Bullfinch, redpoll, linnet, goldfinch, greenfinch, chaffinch, tree sparrow
Groundsel (*Senecio vulgaris*)	Goldfinch, greenfinch
Sorrels (*Rumex spp*)	Linnet, yellowhammer, redpoll
Knotgrass, bistort, red leg (*polygonum spp*)	Linnet, greenfinch, chaffinch
Fat hen (*Chenopodium album*)	Goldfinch, linnet, greenfinch, bullfinch
Sow thistles (*Sonchus spp*)	Bullfinch, goldfinch

Seeds of rank vegetation

Knapweed/Hardhead (*Centaurea nigra*)	Siskin, goldfinch
Meadowsweet (*Filipendula ulmaria*)	Bullfinch, redpoll, siskin, linnet
Thistles (*Carduum & Circium spp*)	Siskin, goldfinch

(Note: garden thistle varieties are just as good and more controllable)

Teasel (*Dipsacus fullonum*)	Goldfinch
Figwort (*Scrophularia nodosa*)	Goldfinch
Seeds of large grasses	Yellowhammer
Docks (*Rumex spp*)	Siskin, linnet, bullfinch
Stinging nettles (*Urtica dioica*)	Bullfinch
Ragwort (*Senecio jacobaea*)	Goldfinch
Dog's mercury (*Mercurialis perennis*)	Greenfinch

Wild berry-bearing weeds and creepers

Blackberry (*Rubus spp*)	Thrushes, warblers, greenfinch, bullfinch, yellowhammer, many others
Woody nightshade (*Solanum dulcamara*)	
Black bryony (*Tamus communis*)	Whitethroat, blackcap, thrushes
White bryony (*Bryonia dioica*)	
Wild arum (*Arum maculatum*)	Blackbird, whitethroat, song thrush

Supplies of seeds of some of these plants, and a wide range of other wildflowers which are beneficial to wildlife are readily obtainable. One good supplier is the Henry Doubleday Research Association (National Centre for Organic Gardening, Ryton-on-Dunsmore, Coventry CV8 3LG); write for a catalogue.

Breeding seasons of garden nesting birds

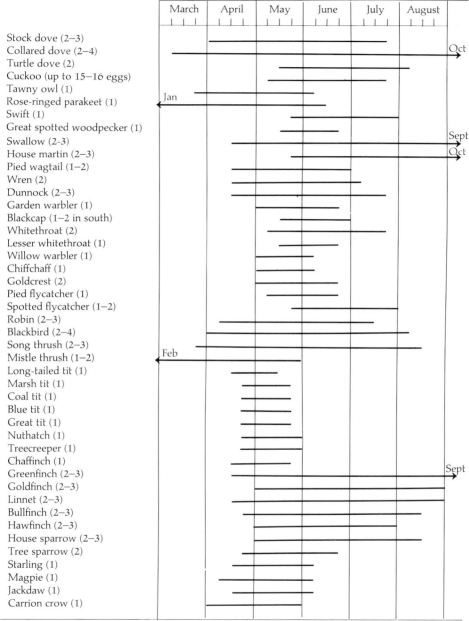

Stock dove (2–3)
Collared dove (2–4)
Turtle dove (2)
Cuckoo (up to 15–16 eggs)
Tawny owl (1)
Rose-ringed parakeet (1)
Swift (1)
Great spotted woodpecker (1)
Swallow (2-3)
House martin (2–3)
Pied wagtail (1–2)
Wren (2)
Dunnock (2–3)
Garden warbler (1)
Blackcap (1–2 in south)
Whitethroat (2)
Lesser whitethroat (1)
Willow warbler (1)
Chiffchaff (1)
Goldcrest (2)
Pied flycatcher (1)
Spotted flycatcher (1–2)
Robin (2–3)
Blackbird (2–4)
Song thrush (2–3)
Mistle thrush (1–2)
Long-tailed tit (1)
Marsh tit (1)
Coal tit (1)
Blue tit (1)
Great tit (1)
Nuthatch (1)
Treecreeper (1)
Chaffinch (1)
Greenfinch (2–3)
Goldfinch (2–3)
Linnet (2–3)
Bullfinch (2–3)
Hawfinch (2–3)
House sparrow (2–3)
Tree sparrow (2)
Starling (1)
Magpie (1)
Jackdaw (1)
Carrion crow (1)

Notes:

1. Breeding season as shown is taken from *average* dates of first laying (south of England) to approximate fledging of last brood. For seasons in northern England and Scotland start one week to ten days later.

2. The usual number of broods reared in a season is shown in brackets. There will be many exceptions; for example in good years single brooded species may suddenly nest twice; some individual pairs of single-brooded species (blue tit, great tit) may produce two broods in any given season.

Winged predators

A garden well supplied with food in the winter and full of breeding birds in the summer will always be attractive to bird predators. In the same way that the song birds will be lured by the food and shelter provided for them so will the predators be drawn to the concentration of potential bird prey. The problem of coming to terms with garden bird predators is a difficult and delicate one for many people. We find it painful mainly because we tend to look upon familiar song birds such as robins, blackbirds and goldfinches as 'nice', and in a sense, our guests desirable; anything which kills them or robs their nests of eggs and young is regarded as 'nasty' and undesirable. Perhaps the sentiment is easy to appreciate but the morals and the logic surrounding it quickly break down when we look at them. Spotted flycatchers kill tortoiseshells and comma butterflies; cuckoos eat furry caterpillars; blackbirds devour miles of worms and we find nothing objectionable while at the same time we dislike the beautiful jay because it takes flycatcher or blackbird eggs. In winter we do what we can to attract the colourful, exciting great spotted woodpecker onto the bird table and in spring we castigate it for taking the blue tit brood from the nest box. Predators and prey live in balance with each other and it is important to remember that the prey species benefit as much from the culling as the predator does by eating them, even if it doesn't do the particular individual that is being eaten an awful lot of good. It is quite literally the survival of the fittest, the fastest, the strongest and most successful – they are the ones that will avoid predation and form the breeding population each year. It is an old adage but perfectly true that 'it is the numbers of prey that determine the numbers of predators, not the reverse'. In a situation of natural balance predators

Jays are one of several species which are fond of 'anting'.

74

do not actually control the numbers of prey, but simply harvest the annual surplus. Nor is this sort of predation cruel in the sense that we normally understand it.

Several members of the crow family are inveterate garden nest robbers. Magpie, jay and carrion crow are the worst offenders but jackdaws and rooks will also empty nests if they happen upon them. The first three are wily and skilled nest finders and account for a lot of nest looting between them. Carrion crows are the least likely in most gardens unless they are really extensive because crows are mainly birds of woodland and open farmland. Here they wreak havoc with lapwing, pheasant, moorhen and other birds of similar size. Magpies and jays will search methodically for nests along the garden hedgerows and in the shrubbery and do a lot of their searching in the very early mornings long before you are awake to see or hear them. It is the open-nest species — blackbird, song thrush, dunnock, collared dove, greenfinch — that are at greatest risk, but their skill certainly extends to include the more secretive nests of willow warbler, robin and coal tit. Jays are equally expert, and both species are adept at watching parent birds back to the nest thus revealing its whereabouts so that they can slip in and plunder. They will do the same by watching human nest visitors so once again think hard about the wisdom of a daily peep in the nests 'to see how they are doing' and thereby beating a path to them, because each visit will increase the chances of the nests failing.

One thought which may console is that many of your garden birds will repeat their nesting attempt if the first one fails and a lot of them are at least double-brooded in any case. If the spring and summer are fine and warm and there is a good supply of natural food, a pair of blackbirds or song thrushes may sometimes have as many as four broods in the year. If the predator thought remains too difficult for you, note that all the crow species mentioned here can be shot or otherwise legally killed at any time of year. Other than this there is little remedial action you can take. Jays are usually silent in the garden but magpies are conversational and chatter to each other in raucous voices which can act as useful alarm clocks for the sleeping bird gardener; one shout or bang on the window will usually despatch them for the morning, for they are shy as well as wary birds. This will not guarantee to save the blackbird's nests however because a birds'-nesting magpie can also be a stealthy and silent hunter.

The local tawny owl may levy a toll of birds from the garden and is certainly not averse to taking nestlings or even adult birds if the chance is offered. Most of the predation obviously occurs at night when roosting birds are taken, so the actual amount is never known but is not likely to be very great. The most regular predation may well take place in towns and cities where roosting starlings and house sparrows are an easy target for a night hunter. Little owls are abroad both by day and night and are partial to young nestlings if they happen upon them but they are not systematic or regular in the habit and the number they take will not usually be significant.

Most of us welcome the sight of a kestrel hovering nearby, secure in the knowledge that it is feeding on a diet of mice and voles. Urban kestrels do not find small rodents as plentiful as they are in the open countryside and many of them become bird hunting specialists. Their main urban prey is starlings and house sparrows but they can become adept at raiding bird tables in search of a wider choice of fare. If they choose to come to your bird table for this purpose there is not a lot you can do to deter them so you may just as well enjoy the privilege of having them in your garden!

The great spotted woodpecker is regarded by most people as one of the prizes to attract to the winter bird table, and it is indeed a striking and colourful bird. Unfortunately it is not the paragon we would think it and in the breeding season many individuals turn to thuggery and murder. A woodpecker's powerful bill can make short work of a soft-wood nest box and they will rapidly enlarge the hole until they can reach inside to take and eat the nestlings. This is not only distressing but also annoying in that it largely destroys the nest box — or at least involves replacing one whole side. The remedy for this problem is to nail a strong metal plate with a hole of the right diameter over the nest box entrance. If it is not easy to produce one locally the RSPB can sell you one.

Several other avian predators may turn up in the garden as rare visitors; perhaps a great grey shrike in autumn, a merlin (we know one town centre in Wales where they hunt regularly) or barn owl. The garden bird-catcher *par excellence* however is the sparrowhawk.

Sparrowhawks and the numbers game

Although a common species — as it now is in most wooded parts of the country — the sparrowhawk is a secretive bird, not easily seen and often then only as a grey-brown shape disappearing fast and low into the trees or scudding down a hedgerow

Garden feeding stations will attract sparrowhawks to the
ready supply of small birds. However, such depredations are
a part of the natural control of populations.

and flitting quickly through a gap to the other side. It is the predator that strikes dread into small birds more than any other, and with good reason for its prey is entirely made up of small birds from the tiniest in size up to those as large as a pigeon. As is the case with all birds of prey the female is bigger than the male (usually a third bigger and twice as heavy) and can therefore take the larger prey. This is a specialist in fast low-level attack and its hunting methods are a combination of stealth, agility and speed. A hunting sparrowhawk will first locate feeding flocks of birds and assess the prospects either by sitting patiently in a vantage tree or circling high over the area. Having once identified the target it then chooses the most covered line of approach and moves in fast just above ground level with alternating powerful wingbeats and long glides. If the approach is a good one the sparrowhawk will only be seen at the last moment, travelling at high speed and the unsuspecting individual which has been singled out has little time to escape the long outstretched leg and needle sharp talons as the sparrowhawk flashes by and flies off with the victim.

If sparrowhawks eat nothing but birds, how many do they need? Females require more than males but in general an adult will have to catch about 2 oz (56 g) of bird meat per day (although the liveweight of the kills is about twice that weight). This is equivalent to two or three chaffinches or one starling or blackbird. It is an easy calculation from there to work out that a pair of sparrowhawks between them will need to catch 1,500–1,600 small birds in the course of a year, *not* including the extra they find to feed a brood. Take it further if you want and bear in mind that there is a minimum of at least 100,000 sparrowhawks in Britain at any time of year and certainly a lot more than that in the months following the breeding season. A simple calculation will give you a rough estimate of the sort of figure which is involved in total sparrowhawk kills over a twelve month period.

A sparrowhawk may well habituate to visiting your bird table but if so try to be philosophical about it. There is no real means by which you can dissuade it (sparrowhawks are especially protected under the Wildlife and Countryside Act 1981) and whatever the toll it takes remember that it is insignificant compared to the numbers of adult and young garden birds which will die during the winter. Earlier in the book we wrote about the number of dunnocks which are destined to die in the course of the year. The numbers game can be employed in the context of sparrowhawks and

their prey – take blue tits for example. A blue tit territory in woodland or garden will be about an acre in size. A decent sized brood from one pair in a year will be about ten and an elderly pair of blue tits might live and breed for five years. Over that period if they and all their successive offspring survived and bred each year, then by the end of the five year period the total number of blue tits would be . . . well, work it out for yourself but it's somewhere in the order of 15,000; all to fit into one acre? So, unless you want to wade knee deep through blue tits in your garden, say a hearty 'thank you' to the sparrowhawk.

Swifts – the devil birds

In the warmth of the summer evenings as dusk approaches, and in the brightness of early morning, the parties of screaming swifts hurtle through the sky above the rooftops and gardens. Their sheer pace and the brilliance of their high-speed aerobatic manoeuvres are astonishing. Of all the birds none has achieved such mastery of the air as the swift. Quite simply swifts live their whole lives on the wing in a way which no other bird has attained. With long, narrow, scimitar-shaped wings and small body the swift is designed as the perfect high speed endurance flier. The air is the swift's complete element supplying all its needs. Only the fact that once it is mature it has to come to land to actually lay the eggs, incubate them and then feed the unfledged young, causes it ever to leave its element. The swift feeds on tiny flies which it catches on the wing. On good days when the insects have risen in the warm air the swifts hunt them high above the rooftops but on heavy overcast or thundery days when the insects are at ground level they are forced lower to skim above the grassy meadows and playing fields and search for them there. Swifts also drink, bathe and even 'sleep' on the wing. Water is taken either as rain or occasionally by dipping into the surface of lakes and rivers and they will 'bathe' as other birds do but in their case by seeking out and flying through showers of rain. During the time when they have eggs or young the parent swifts usually roost together in the nest but non-breeding birds, and all swifts at other times of year, roost high in the sky. Shortly before nightfall they will leave and if you are observant and prepared to put up with a crick in the neck, use a pair of binoculars and watch them rise higher and higher in the darkening sky. Far above the towns and villages they will slowly circle the night away, riding the air currents and 'cat-napping' for a few seconds at a time, opening their eyes to re-adjust and then dropping off again.

Nesting materials in the form of floating feathers and small wind-blown straws of grass are collected in May and June and cemented together with saliva to make the nest, and swifts have even evolved the ultimate refinement of mating on the wing. A swift's enemies are few. Hobbies are capable of catching them by sheer speed and peregrines too but the number taken is small and the one serious live enemy is ironically the tiny flightless louse-fly (see page 69) which infests the birds and their nests and accounts for numbers of deaths. The most serious natural hazard for an airborne bird is bad weather. Continual rain and cold can mean serious food shortage and rapid debilitation, and certainly in their tropical winter homes they are sometimes known to be caught out by sudden storms and literally knocked out of the sky.

July comes and the swifts prepare to leave. After some six weeks in the nest the swiftlets hesitate in the opening for a day or two, stretching and strengthening their untried wings and waiting to take the ultimate plunge. Ultimate it is, because from this plunge there is no return and no second chance. Encouraged by the calling and the swooping visits of the parents the young swifts eventually drop out into the unknown. If they get it wrong it has been a short life indeed, entirely confined to a space in the roof, and now they will end up marooned on the ground as prey for cats and owls. If they have put it all together properly and fly off high into the sky it may well be three years before their wings stop beating and they touch down again, three years during which they will live entirely on the wing.

How fast then does a swift fly and how far may it travel in its lifetime? In level-flight they can comfortably exceed seventy miles per hour and in short bursts they probably approach ninety miles per hour. Swifts are relatively long-lived birds and the mileage they cover in their lifetime is prodigious. One often-quoted swift is known to have lived for over sixteen years during which time it is suggested that it probably covered something like five million miles! That is 200 circuits of the globe or the equivalent of ten return trips to the moon.

It is little wonder that the swift has always been surrounded by mystery and suspense, living a life of which we see nothing more than a summer glimpse and which has many aspects that are actually difficult for us to comprehend. For long it was understandably known as the 'Devil's bird' or 'Devil's screacher'.

An ingenuous song thrush just out of the nest is ready prey for any garden predator.

JULY

Looking after feathers

The care of feathers is a critical part of every bird's daily maintenance programme. However cold it is on a winter's day or however insistently the young family calls for food in the summer, the vital business of preening and keeping the feathers in good condition must be fitted in sometime. As well as giving birds the power of flight, its feathers are also the means of insulating and helping control the body temperature. Bedraggled feathers waste body heat and make for inefficient flying, and in winter lost body heat is not easily replaced. The first key to this servicing of feathers is regular bathing, followed up by re-proofing and finishing off with careful manicuring. The bird bath and the garden pond are focal points in the bird's daily life and they will be used more in the holidays of July and August than at any other time. Birds bathe energetically, splashing and shaking themselves in the water until the plumage is thoroughly wetted. The aim is to wet the plumage without actually soaking it, thereby making it more receptive to the oiling and preening which follow. Water is splashed well into the feathers to wash out the dust, scales and parasites which accumulate there. The water is then squeezed out to the surface and shaken off as the bird dries itself.

The blackbird is a great bather; watch it as it shows off the feathers to best advantage at bathing time: with wings outspread the handsome tail is held down at a right angle and fanned wide to show it full spread.

Once the bathing is finished the bird begins to preen. Twisting its tail to the side it reaches down over its back and collects the waterproofing oil with its bill from the preen gland near the base of its tail and carefully wipes the oil onto its body feathers and wings. In between times it will take individual feathers in its bill and very gently stroke them back into shape, zipping together the individual barbs and tiny barbules which have been ruffled and displaced during the day's activities. So water-bathing, oiling and preening are the key parts of feather servicing but they are not the only maintenance activities you may see if you are observant in the summer garden

'Anting' — home-made insect spray?

By mid-summer most of the birds breeding in the garden have seen their young safely out of the nest and for many of them it is probably the quietest and least stressful time throughout the whole of the bird year. At this time some species indulge in the strange habit of 'anting'. It is commonest among members of the crow family but in the garden it is most likely to be either starling, blackbird or song thrush that you will see, although chaffinch and one or two other common species of song birds are also known to do it on occasions.

This is an odd activity in which the bird will

Regular bathing is a crucial part of daily feather care.

Wren sunbathing: the warmth of the sun helps put feathers back in their original shape.

seek out an active ants' nest, pick up ants one by one with the tip of the bill and appear to wipe them along the underside of the wing, mainly on the outer flight feathers. Each ant is crushed before being wiped along the feathers in a fast, flicking action; it is then dropped and another one is picked up. During the performance the bird strikes a special 'anting' posture, usually with one wing raised and tail fanned. This type of activity is called 'active anting' but as an alternative birds will sometimes also go in for passive anting in which they stand among the milling ants with wings and tail spread wide and let the angry insects run all over their plumage; if necessary the bird will stir the ants up a bit to make them even more active!

Of all our common species the jay is the one most frequently recorded anting and it also 'ants' in a different way to the standard one described, arching both wings forward like a tent in front of its lowered head. The jay swarms with ants in no time, quivering and shuddering as they run all over it in barely concealed irritation.

Scientists have argued for a long time about the reasons why birds should behave in such a strange way with ants. The most popular theory is that they are doing it as part of the vital work of keeping feathers in perfect condition. The formic acid and anal fluids exuded by the ants are insecticidal and applying them to the feathers may well help to control tiny feather parasites. Certainly anting birds frequently preen and bathe immediately afterwards. In addition it may possibly act as a cleaner to help remove old preen-oil from the feathers. Whatever function it is a very odd activity which is likely to have you guessing the first July day that you see it.

Sunning . . .

In the heat of the day in summer birds sometimes find a sheltered hot-spot and instead of keeping in the cool at siesta time as they usually do, they will indulge in a bit of sun-bathing. The chosen spot will usually be on bare ground where there is reflected heat as well, together with nearby shade which will allow them to hide if danger threatens or limit their sun-bathing if they start to overheat.

A sun-bathing bird spreadeagles itself on the ground with wings and tail open wide. This too is all part of the routine maintenance of good feathers. In this case the hot rays of the sun will actually help restore flight feathers to their original shape. It may also help stimulate the flow of preen oil and flush out feather parasites from hidden corners of the plumage into parts where they are more accessible: a special dose of sunshine to reach the parts that other rays can't reach.

... and dust bathing

House sparrows are the keenest dust bathers among our garden birds. In summer they love to find an area of really fine sandy soil and produce their own little wallow pits. They wriggle down into the dusty soil and then rub their heads in it, and throw dust up into their body feathers. They ruffle the dust all through their plumage before shaking it out again. Wrens are fairly regular dust bathers as well. Much head scratching and preen-

ing are interspersed with bouts of dust bathing thus identifying it as yet another activity which is a regular and important part of feather maintenance at this time of year. If your garden has heavy soil which is not helpful to dust bathing sparrows or wrens, do not be afraid to supply them with some suitable sandy or dusty soil yourself for they will surely find it and use it. Give the dust bath a quick dose of Poultry Aerosol or Cooper's Household Insect Powder every now and then if you think of it, for the general good of the bathers.

Birds and window panes

One of the bird hazards of modern houses is the large windows which are frequently fitted. All too often, particularly on bright days, they reflect the clouds and the sky and can confuse birds in the garden outside, causing them to fly into the glass. Equally bad news for birds are big picture windows with another window at the opposite end of the room giving the impression of a

Feather care is a daily task: a treecreeper manicures its tail feathers back into shape.

House sparrows (male in the foreground) are the most frequent dust bathers.

fly-way straight through; glass conservatories can have the same effect.

July and August are the times when accidents of this sort are most likely to happen with a garden full of young inexperienced birds. It is the youngsters that make up the majority of these casualties and although the list of those species which have been involved is almost as long as the list of garden birds itself, several species are regular casualties. Warblers of many sorts seem particularly prone; whitethroat, willow warbler, blackcap are notable. Juvenile thrushes and blackbirds too are very vulnerable as are kingfishers on occasions (four on one window one year) and young dunnocks and robins. The list doesn't stop at small birds. Mrs Williams of Ludlow in Shropshie had a double surprise when she heard a window pane shatter and ran into the sitting room to find a dying blackbird in the armchair and an angry and bemused female sparrowhawk glaring at her from the middle of the carpet. We have also heard of a pheasant going straight through a closed window and there must be other householders who can add to the list.

Normally of course the injury is to the bird and not the window. Frequently its neck is broken in the impact and it is killed outright, but as often as not when you hear the bang on the pane and run outside you will find the casualty lying stunned but not dead. In this case take the bird carefully inside and keep it in a warm place in a small closed cardboard box or similar, ensuring that plenty of air can circulate through it. Within a short while you will find that the bird is either recovered and can be released outside or it has succumbed and died.

Fortunately there are several things which can be done to avoid or at least reduce the casualty list. If the problem windows are in a room which you do not use regularly consider drawing the curtains at the offending end to cut out the reflection; it is a trick that will work where birds have been able to see straight through opposite windows. Affixing a cut-out flight silhouette of a kestrel or sparrowhawk made from black paper on to the window pane also serves well to keep small birds away. Net curtains will greatly improve the situation and another idea is to place a tall house plant by the inside of the window during the vulnerable months. Of course you could always keep your windows dirty in July and August, that would do the trick too!

Herons and the goldfish pond

Herons must see goldfish ponds as being put there especially for them; their equivalent of a 'choose-your-own' live-fish restaurant. The sight of a wild grey heron poised in the shallows above the unsuspecting goldfish is momentarily thrilling and then probably galling. The trouble is that you don't often see the bird itself, you simply find a reducing stock of fish and eventually an empty pond because the heron's main feeding time is in the first light of dawn before most of us are about. The RSPB receives frequent enquiries from people whose fish ponds are being raided by herons taking advantage of an easy meal. The problem also exists on fish farms and RSPB research aimed at trying to find effective deterrents has produced some results that are applicable to garden ponds too. The following is the advice which the RSPB gives.

'Herons will usually land next to a pond and then walk to the edge, where they will either reach down into the water, or if it is shallow enough, wade into it. Given the small size of garden ponds it is sometimes possible to net over the entire pond, but this can be impractical and unsightly. A simpler deterrent is the use of a barrier of height 14 in (35 cm), placed around the edge of the pond. A wire fence can be used, but a simple "trip-wire" at this height, with another underneath it at a height of 8 in (20 cm) should suffice. Strong polypropylene twine would be suitable and silver paper, bells or other scaring devices can be attached to it.

If you are constructing an ornamental fish pond then by making the sides vertical, and keeping the water level at least 35 cm below ground level, you will deny access to the herons. Sloping banks will be better for small birds, which can drink and bathe, and also for amphibians.

Please remember that herons, their nests and eggs are afforded full legal protection'.

In addition to these suggestions, if you can bear the sight of a model heron or similar bird stuck on the side of your pond, it is worth trying and it will probably deter wild herons for a while because they like to feed exclusively and will avoid a small pond if they see an engaged sign up.

Fortunately, the problem of herons and garden ponds is a seasonal one, usually restricted to young birds in late summer and autumn.

Garden ponds

No wildlife garden is complete without a decent pond. It doesn't have to be big to be exciting, but of course the larger you are able to make it, the better. Other than the installation of a bird feeding table there is no feature you can produce in your garden that will bring such a quick return; in fact the pond will score hand-over-fist in all-round terms because of the wide variety of other wildlife it will attract. There may be some hard work involved in making yourself a pond but the amount of pleasure you will get from it will comfortably outweigh a few blisters and some sore arms. Even if your garden is very small, resist the temptation of avoiding the hard work by buying a readymade plastic or fibreglass pond from your garden centre because in this instance you can almost certainly do a more satisfactory job yourself and build it to the exact specification you need. There are innumerable plans and patterns for garden ponds available nowadays and the outlines we suggest here have endless variants. Most good gardening books give information and advice as do the county Naturalists' Trusts and the main national conservation bodies. Advice is not in short supply for pond diggers! Provided the ground is not too hard to dig, July or August is quite a good time to start pond work. Soil is much easier to handle and move than when it is cloggy and wet in winter and it will certainly make less general mess. It will also give you plenty of time to complete the pond, let it settle and then start to establish some of the waterside plants in the period of autumn planting. Once you have determined to add a pond to your garden, follow the suggested steps set out here. They should apply to your pond whatever size you are hoping to make.

1. Think, plan and decide. Consider the best place in the garden from the point of view of the wildlife using it, as well as from your own outlook and need to be able to watch birds and others from the house. Make sure it will be in good sunlight so that aquatic plants and insects can thrive and not under trees where it would suffer heavy leaf fall in autumn and become clogged. Think carefully about the most suitable size of pond for the garden and be satisfied that you have a level site to build it on. Decide whether you are going to build a concrete-lined pond (which will need quite a lot

In late summer or autumn young herons may explore the garden pond.

more digging out) or one using a plastic liner. As ever, ensure that the pond will not put bathing or drinking birds at risk from cats lurking in ready-made hiding places too close by. Finally don't forget that you need to have somewhere to put all the soil you dig out from the pond; so many pond diggers underestimate the number of barrow loads even a small hole will produce.

2. Peg out the pond and dig it out. Mark the edges of the pond with wooden pegs and remember that if you are working on ground which is not quite level you will need to put the shallowest end down slope. Use a long plank with a spirit level to check. It is important to keep within the pegs you have set out and not let enthusiasm run wild once you get the spade in your hands, or you will suddenly realise that your carefully measured liner

will no longer fit the hole! Now you are ready to start the hard work. Take off the turves and keep them to one side for later use; keep the good top soil nearby as well because you will need it to return to the bottom of the pond afterwards. Dispose of the subsoil or use the best of it to make some other garden feature. All the edges of the pond should be very shallow slopes so that they can be used in perfect safety by bathing and drinking birds and can give easy 'walk-in' access to frogs, toads and other pond animals. Even if you are digging a large pond it should nowhere be any deeper than 30 in (75 cm), and if it is of very modest size the deep part should probably not exceed 18 in (45 cm). When digging out remember to take into account that you have to put several inches of top soil back once the liner is in

It is a lucky garden where the pond is occasionally visited by a kingfisher.

place. If space permits, it is a good idea to allow for a marshy area at the shallowest side of the pond. To do this excavate the soil to a depth of about 2 in (5 cm) over the selected area.

3. Lining the pond. You will have decided beforehand whether to concrete the pond or to use a liner. Concreting will be heavy work (and deeper excavating) and seems an unnecessary labour nowadays. If you do concrete however, make it about 6 in (15 cm) thick and then seal it with bitumen paint or special waterproof cement. By far the simplest and most effective method of lining is to use one of the several types of pond liner which are readily available from good garden centres or plastic suppliers. Do not use anything thinner than 1,000 gauge (15/1,000 in) or it will be too easily punctured. Thick black polythene can be used but is not particularly durable and does not have a life of more than five years or so, especially in sunlight. It is relatively cheap but is probably not a good buy for your needs. PVC sheeting is better and has a longer life-expectancy, and the best type is that which is strengthened with nylon. Polyolefin is another alternative with a use-life of some fifteen years or more and either of these two will do the job well for you. However, as you are going to the time and trouble of making a pond

only once it is worth considering the most expensive but certainly the best type of liner, that made of butyl rubber. It is thick but flexible, has a life of well over fifteen years and does not puncture as easily as the cheaper plastic alternatives.

Once you have completed the digging remove any stones in the bottom which may puncture the liner and then put a thick layer of newspaper or soft sand over the whole area before laying the butyl or plastic on top. Spread the liner and push it gently into the shape of the hole not making any attempt to straighten it or pull it tight, but making sure that there is plenty of slack. The weight of the water will eventually make it fit snugly into all the contours and pull it tight for you. Leave generous overlaps around the edge for the time being and weigh it down temporarily here and there with smooth heavy stones. Make sure you do not tread on it or do anything else which will risk puncturing it.

4. Replace the soil. It is best now to fill the pond with water and leave it for a few days. If you have made mistakes with levelling or have sprung a leak now is the time to find out rather than later. Water levels at the shallowest end should give you a depth varying from $\frac{3}{4}$ in (2 cm) to 4 in (10 cm). Once the liner has had two or three days to settle,

86

carefully cut off all the surplus plastic remembering to leave 8–10in (20–25 cm) overlap beyond the top water edge and not forgetting to ensure that the 'marshy patch' is also well covered. If you cut the liner too soon you may be in trouble as it tends to shrink and be drawn into the pool as the weight of water slowly presses it into its final position.

Use the turves you first took off the site to put on top of the exposed edge of the sheet all round the pond (or use slabs, stones or whatever best suits you). It is important to ensure that all bits of sheeting are well covered as it will otherwise deteriorate in the direct sunlight. Take the topsoil you kept to one side and scatter it all over the surface of the pond so that it sinks to the bottom to make a uniform silty bed of at least 3–4 in (7.5–10 cm) depth. At the shallow end this will produce the wet mud for your marshy area. Place one or two large stones or a log in the water if you wish so that they stick up just above the surface or lie just below it; birds will use these freely to land on and drink. Leave the whole thing a couple of weeks or so to settle, and for the water to start to clear. Add a couple of buckets of water from a nearby pond to introduce the necessary microorganisms. Keep it topped up with the hosepipe if there is no rain to do the job for you and make sure that the overflow is dealing with any excess properly. Your pond is now ready for planting!

If the soil in the pond is in contact with the dry garden soil beyond it is likely that you will lose quite a lot of water by capillary action in hot, dry weather, so this is a point to watch out for also.

Plants for the pond

A garden pond must be stocked with the correct plants if it is going to support the wide range of wildlife of which it is capable. Apart from directly providing plant food for water insects and other invertebrates (water snails etc) they will also absorb the carbon dioxide produced by the small animals living in the water and release vital oxygen. Pond plants can conveniently be put into three categories and you should make sure that your pond has some of each: free floating, bottom-rooted, marginal/marshy edge plants.

Free floating plants may best be obtained by persuading neighbours to spare you a bucketful from their pond or knowing a pond locally where the farmer will give you permission. The most important plants in this group are all well known and common species in ponds and canals but remember that it offends many people's conservation principles nowadays to see plants being taken from the wild and put in gardens. If in doubt and your neighbours cannot help you, go to your water garden nurseryman again. The key species to choose should come from the following which are all important oxygenators.

Duckweed (*Lemna* spp)
Water violet (*Hottonia palustris*) – nectar-rich
   flowers for insects too.
Frogbit (*Hydrocharis morus-ranae*)
Hornwort (*Ceratophyllum demersum*) – deep
   living, not on surface; sometimes rooting.
Water fern (*Azolla filiculoides*)
Water soldier (*Stratiotes aloides*) – an underwater

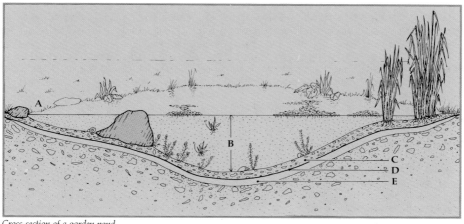

Cross-section of a garden pond.
KEY
A Replaced turfs   **C** Top soil   **E** Sand or newspaper
B Depth 18 in (45 cm)   **D** Poly lining

Frogs in the garden pond.

plant; surfaces at flowering time.
Starwort (*Callitriche palustris*)

A good way of establishing bottom-rooting plants is to set them in specially made plastic pots in good soil and lower them on to the pond bottom rather than trying to anchor them in the loose mud; alternatively try weighting them down with stones etc. Try a few plants of white water lily (*Nymphaea alba*) – but they can spread quite fast – reed mace (*Typha latifolia*) – which also needs keeping under control – or *Ottelia alismoides* which has white emergent flowers while the long green leaves remain permanently submerged.

There are plenty of marshy edge plants from which to choose. Keep a place for meadowsweet because it is one of the few marsh plants which has seeds attractive to birds.

Otherwise select from some of the following:
Marsh marigold (*Caltha palustris*) : golden flowers, March–June.
Brooklime (*Veronica beccabunga*) : May–September.
Watermint (*Mentha aquatica*) : July–September.
Water forget-me-not (*Myosotis* spp) : June–August.
Spike rush (*Eleocharis acicularis*) : good seed for mallard and moorhen.
Water plantain (*Alisma plantago-aquatica*)

Once again try to persuade neighbours to let you have a few of their plants to start you off or get them from the nursery. Do not dig them up from the wild.

Pond animals

It is always surprising how pond animals will find their own way into your new water world so quickly. All the same there is a lot to be said for introducing some common water snails as quickly as possible to graze the algae that develops. Once again it's probably a case of scrounging from the long-suffering neighbours for a handful but alternatively your aquarist will be happy to sell them to you. They will probably find their own population balance at about one snail for every 2 sq in (5 sq cm) of water surface, so don't overstock to start with. Frogs and toads are best initiated by introducing the spawn of either of them in early spring. Beware of introducing newts if your pond is very small (they will probably find their own way in the end anyway) because they will eat almost anything they can lay hands on. Water beetles, spiders and water boatmen can easily be recruited from the local canal or pond. Dragonflies and pond skaters will certainly find your new water themselves in a very short time. If your pond is small it is best to steer clear of any fish but if it is large you can introduce still-water fish to suit your whim. Bear in mind that goldfish are bottom feeders and tend to make the pond muddy all the time (but at least the herons may thank you!). Minnows will help control the mosquito and gnat larvae which are bound to turn up and these small fish may even attract a kingfisher if your garden is near other water: place an over-hanging branch or other perch 3 ft (90 cm) above the minnows favourite area if you want to lure the kingfisher in. (Avoid sticklebacks, however.)

With your pond complete you can sit back and enjoy it. Whether or not the kingfisher comes, robins, thrushes, sparrows and starlings will come to bathe and drink. In dry weather wood pigeons and collared doves or the shy jay may come too, and the bright green woodpecker or even the sparrowhawk. Birds will interact with the other pond life too: blackbirds will hunt for tadpoles and spotted flycatchers pursue the dragonflies. If you have got things right the pond will need minimum maintenance other than to clean out dead leaves from time to time or cut back the bullrush or water lily. It will bring endless entertainment and interest.

Protecting soft fruit

Ripening soft fruit and swelling rows of peas make easy targets for birds in July and there are many

beaks that will take first pick of the harvest before you have had the opportunity to gather it your-self. Blackbirds and song thrushes will regularly take strawberries and raspberries; linnets will sometimes acquire the habit of feeding on the external seeds and spoiling strawberries and house sparrows and even turtle doves will sometimes do the same. Jays, (and if you are very lucky, haw-finches!) will strip a row of peas in the kitchen garden in the early mornings and magpies, jays or carrion crows will demolish a crop of gooseber-ries, especially the big dessert leveller varieties.

Generations of gardeners have wrestled with the problems of bird damage using whole armou-ries of bird scares, scarecrows, networks of black cotton, rustling tin foil and children's cellophane windmills. All of them may work in the short term but birds rapidly get used to them and call your bluff. It may be worth trying a bird of prey flight model on a pole above a vulnerable crop. A fairly inocuous chemical repellent, anthraquinone, is obtainable as a bird deterrent on fruit *buds* but not the fruit itself.

Nowadays when durable lightweight netting is available everywhere on the roll, surely the only answer for protecting these vulnerable crops is to enclose them in netting on light pole frames? It is not too expensive and does the job once and for all. In winter it has the advantage that you can move it and protect the greens from the wood-pigeons in the same way.

The ubiquitous house sparrow is one of the most cosmopolitan and successful garden birds.

Spotted flycatchers are late arrivals, timing things so that
there are good numbers of large flying insects on the wing
once they are here.

90

AUGUST

ugust – the dog days and summer doldrums. It is now as quiet a time of year as there will be in the garden. Apart from last broods of collared dove, goldfinch, house martin or blackbird, the breeding season is over for most, although the beginning of autumn activity is still several weeks away. Birds are quiet and unobtrusive and it is the nearest that one will get to identifying an ending-and-a-beginning to the bird year. For the gardener and the garden birdwatcher it is probably the time for rest and holiday too; a time to look elsewhere and break from the demands of the garden. Let us quietly accept that this is not the most exciting time of the year!

New feathers for old

High summer, the end of the breeding season and parent birds are worn out and jaded. It is a time for rest and recovery and above all else a time to shed the old feathers which have done duty now for twelve months and replace them with a new set. Gap-winged rooks and carrion crows have been flying around for several weeks now, labouring in the wind with exaggerated and inefficient wing beats. Ducks retreat into thick waterside vegetation because unlike other birds, but in common with geese and swans, they lose all their flight feathers simultaneously and are completely flightless for about four weeks; when they do fly again the season's offspring will have developed their wing feathers and will fly with them for the first time.

Garden birds are enthusiastic bathers in July and August as the accumulation of summer parasites, dust and general dirt irritates them and the dilapidated state of feathers makes matters worse. These tired breeding birds can look sadly dishevelled at this time of year with feathers missing, tips broken and dulled plumage in disarray. Moult is itself a stressful process and requires extra food and body energy. Blackbirds show their moulting pattern well at this time of year: note how they shed their head feathers last of all with the result that young ones appear ginger-headed before the moult is complete.

Birds are especially vulnerable to predators at this time and they become shy, secretive and unobtrusive. Although the bird population in the garden is now higher than at any other time of year, swollen by the progeny of the breeding season, most of the birds are skulking and withdrawn and one might be forgiven for imagining that the garden is almost bare of birds. The timing of the moult for our resident garden species is not nearly as critical as it is for the migratory ones. Migrants must either complete the moult of wing and tail feathers before departing or delay until after they arrive at their winter home. Most will in fact complete the moult before departure and have strong new feathers for their long journeys, but swallows are one species which will not start to moult until they eventually reach their winter destination in southern Africa. The willow warbler actually moults twice, once here before it flies south in autumn, and once in Africa before the return journey to us next spring.

Wing and tail feathers are usually shed pair by pair in this post-breeding moult until all are successively replaced over a period of a few weeks. They are shed evenly, one from the right side and one from the left so that reasonable balance is maintained for flight during the moult. The new feathers appear as sheathed buds protruding from the follicles in the skin and, nourished by an enriched blood supply, these 'feather buds' rapidly lengthen and eventually split to allow the new feathers to emerge and grow to shape.

Body-contour feathers moult in much the same pattern but this is a slower and more continuous process which may have started during the breeding season and continue through to late summer and early autumn. As ever there are some special strategies employed by particular species. For example the great spotted woodpecker, which relies on its two long central tail feathers as support when climbing, actually retains the old pair until all other tail feathers have been replaced so that it minimises its climbing handicap.

Early departures

Although it is still high summer the first visiting breeders are soon departing on their way south again. The annual timetable of migrating birds is no simple pattern of spring arrivals and autumn departures or vice versa; rather it is a complex and mysterious network of arrivals and departures all through the year. Migration involves so many species and occurs for a variety of purposes that it is actually taking place in one form or another all the time, although spring and autumn of course remain the busiest and most visible seasons of bird migration. Even right through the summer the tide of migration ebbs and flows: the last of the summer breeding birds do not arrive until late May; by then male goosanders, having mated and bred, are already *en route* for northern Finland to moult, leaving the females incubating; in early

A few weeks after leaving the host's nest, juvenile cuckoos will make their solitary way to winter homes in Africa.

June post-breeding parties of Continental lapwings begin to arrive; in July shelduck and scoter fly to moulting grounds and the first of the arctic waders are back on our watersides. Clapham Junction, with one thousand trains per day, has nothing on the non-stop bird corridors of Western Europe.

The swift's stay with us is all too short and suddenly in the early days of August they are no longer there and the sky is silent. They are southbound, heading for the vast savannahs of Zaire and later the cloudless skies of Zimbabwe, Mozambique or Malawi. Adult male cuckoos departed a month earlier, by the end of June. The female may depart about the same time or in some cases linger a little longer to complete egg laying well into July. They too head south of the Equator to a land of frequent rains and endless caterpillars. Neither of the parent cuckoos of course ever set eyes on their youngster growing, gross and incongruous in the dunnock's nest in your garden hedge. Now, in August, another of the miracles of the cuckoo mystery unfolds. A month or more after the adults have left our shores the newly independent youngsters will abruptly leave and head off south-east into Europe. From there, one by one, they make their way further and further south to preordained wintering areas beyond the Sahara, completely unaccompanied and unguided. What instinct guides them to their uncharted destination 3,000 miles away? For that matter how is it that they can return to the same natal area in following springs?

The deadwood stage

Wildlife gardening gives you the perfect excuse to justify a bit of untidiness. Leaf litter, dead flower heads, seeding weeds and plenty of decay are all-important in their various ways to the wide range of insects, animals and birds which make up the wildlife community in the garden. Keep a good compost heap for all the soft stems, vegetable waste and rotting grass; it will grow good worms and lots of other little decomposers which make it a happy hunting ground for robins, blackbirds and song thrushes. Hedgehogs too will use it and if you are lucky slow worms or grass-snakes.

Keep a special place for any decaying timber, either standing trees and stumps, fallen branches or logs. Let them slowly rot down over time and they will be colonised by a whole world of insects, fungi and invertebrates. Birds such as robin, treecreeper, nuthatch, woodpecker and tits will probe the decaying hollows and a miniature garden of mosses and small flowering plants will grow on rotting logs lying on the ground. Small mammals will live in among them and hedgehogs find the hollows beneath them to hibernate. Decaying wood is a must in the bird garden and if you need a useful activity this month and the garden is short

93

Late summer is the time for replacing tired and used feathers.

of dead wood, take the trouble to import some.

The suburban parrot

Be prepared for a quick double-take if you think you see a medium sized green parrot fly fast across the garden, but don't be totally incredulous. Our suburban gardens have been slowly invaded over the past twenty years by a highly unlikely but successful visitor, the rose-ringed parakeet (or ring-necked parakeet as it is also known). As with most other parrots it is a striking and brightly coloured bird, about the body-size of a blackbird but with a long 10 in (25 cm) pointed tail. It is a brilliant yellow-green bird with red bill and eye, and the male has a neat pink-and-black necklace and dusty blue sheen on the back of its head and its tail.

Since the 1960s this improbable foreigner has gained an increasingly secure foothold in our gardens, especially in south-east England. It is a favourite of the pet trade, imported for many years from tropical Africa and India, and the feral population in the London area clearly arose from escaped birds or ones that were deliberately released. Since then it has increased steadily in the Home Counties where it still has its stronghold, but it has been seen in over fifty counties now and has bred as far apart as South Wales, Merseyside, West Yorkshire and North Wales. It is suggested that there are now well over 1,000 free flying in different parts of the country.

The rose-ringed parakeet shows few of the niceties which one might expect of an invited visitor. It is a brash and noisy customer with a loud screeching call — a tropical-forest voice which

In summer, a good spacious lawn provides feeding for green woodpeckers.

seems far out of place in a British garden. Its improbable success is founded on a commendable disregard for the rigours of winter, but it has become heavily dependent on the garden bird table where it is immediately top of the peck order and a willing and omnivorous feeder. In its natural home it takes plant food, mainly fruits, berries, grain, buds and flowers. In late summer and autumn in Britain it feeds extensively on garden fruit trees, especially apples. Unfortunately it is a wasteful eater, taking only one or two pieces from an apple and then dropping it to take another. If it does continue to strengthen its foothold it could well become one of the horticultural pests of the future.

Although gregarious in winter, the parties break up very early and nesting begins from January on. It is a tree-hole nester often taking over the old site of a woodpecker or stockdove. What can you do to attract this colourful extrovert to your garden? Probably not a lot; just keep filling the bird table up and grow a few apples. Sit back and give him a bit longer and he'll get there in the end.

Colour in the plumage

Summer moult will soon renew the worn and faded feathers and produce crisp new sets of plumages involving a host of shades and colours. What produces the sensational colours of a parakeet, the sheen of a magpie's plumage, the calypso colours of a puffin's bill or the subtle tones of a tree-creeper's delicate pattern? There are two principal sources of colours: pigments, and the structure of the feathers themselves.

Pigments are mainly of two types: melanins, which are already present in the body and which produce the range of buffs, browns and black, and carotenoids which are synthesised by body chemistry and give reds, yellows and orange in different shades. The carotenoid pigments are taken in through the bird's diet and account for the parakeet's red bill or the flamingo's rosy flush. Feed a bright yellow canary on paprika and you will change it into a bright red one!

Blues and greens are the result of different patterns in the structure of the tiny barbules on the feathers themselves. Different structure patterns reflect different portions of the spectrum. Blue for example is produced when the surface pattern of the barbules reflects blue light and allows the remainder to pass through. Differing shades of blue or green are produced when the feathers are pigmented with melanins or carotenoids. White is produced when almost all light from the spectrum is reflected.

Garden chemicals

The shelves of garden centres and shops are weighed down with the means for us to wage total chemical warfare against the chosen undesirable weeds and insects in the garden. The bird gardener has difficult decisions to make about the extent to which he will make use of herbicides or pesticides. Certainly there are some which are very specific, have few known side effects on other wildlife and save much time and crop damage. There are plenty on the market however which are non-selective and should on no account be used in the

Imported rose-ringed parakeets are gaudy additions to an increasing number of gardens, especially in south-east England.

caring person's garden: it is salutory to remember that the unwise use of organochlorine chemicals on farmland in the 1950s and 1960s was the greatest single threat to the survival of our wild birds and seriously reduced the populations of a wide range of our farmland birds and especially the predators which feed on them. Never lose sight of the fact that organic gardening principles and the recommended methods of crop protection and insect control which go with them are being increasingly adopted by gardeners. The Henry Doubleday Research Association (National Centre for Organic Gardening, Ryton-on-Dunsmore, Coventry CV8 3LG) can supply you with a comprehensive catalogue and much advice.

The RSPB has given much time and thought in preparing information which may be helpful in choosing and using the garden chemicals which will cause least damage. There are a large number of pesticides for garden use on the market and the chemicals recommended by the RSPB are the active ingredients of products that are sold under a variety of proprietary brand names. After deciding that you really need to use a chemical preparation, check the manufacturer's label carefully to make sure that the product contains the right chemical for the job. The Government's Control of Pesticides Regulations 1986 make it an offence to sell, supply, store, use or advertise an unapproved pesticide. *Pesticides 1986*, published by Her Majesty's Stationery Office lists those products now approved or provisionally approved under these regulations. The following information is extracted from this publication.

'All chemicals should be used with great care. Here are three points to consider before buying them:

1. Only use a pesticide if you can identify what is affecting your plants – it may not be a pest.

2. Pesticides may affect harmless species as well as the pests they are intended for.

3. There is a tendency to use chemicals when pest populations are at their peak, and may decline through natural causes. Use of pesticides at this stage may prolong infestation or kill natural predators such as ladybirds which eat greenfly and other aphids.

Some chemicals can be irritating to skin, eyes and respiratory system. If you *must* use a pesticide then remember that you are using a poisonous substance and take the following precautions:

Always

Obey the manufacturer's instructions.

Wash hands and utensils carefully after use.

Keep chemicals out of reach of children and pets.

Avoid contaminating bird baths, water tanks and particularly ponds, streams and ditches – as fish are susceptible to many chemicals, even when they are diluted.

Avoid spraying plants when they are in flower, to reduce the risks to bees and other pollinating or nectar-feeding insects. If you must spray at this stage, then do so in the evening. Do not spray when there is a risk of the chemical drifting in the wind. This is particularly important when applying herbicides as a fine mist spray can severely affect herbaceous plants.

Only buy the quantity of chemical that you need.

Any special disposal instructions will be given on the label. Detailed advice is contained in the leaflet *Guidelines for the disposal of unwanted pesticides and containers*. Copies can be obtained from the Ministry of Agriculture, Fisheries and Food. Aerosol containers must not be placed on or near a fire as they can be explosive.

Insecticides

Care should be taken that beneficial insects such as bees and ladybirds are not harmed when insecticides are being used. Some chemicals can also have adverse effects on particular plants and you must make sure that the product you are using is suitable.

Specific uses	Recommended treatment
Ants	Pyrethrum
Aphids: on fruits	Spray before blossoming with malathion
on vegetables	Malathion
and ornamental plants	(some plants can be damaged by this: check before use)
Caterpillars on vegetables	Chlorpyrifos
Cabbage fly	Bromophos
Carrot fly	Bromophos
Codling moth	Chlorpyrifos
Cutworms	Bromophos or chlorpyrifos
Onion fly	Bromophos or chlorpyrifos
Raspberry beetle	Derris dust or malathion
Red spider mite	Derris (roses), malathion or chlorpyrifos
Sawflies	Chlorpyrifos
Thrips	Derris (roses) or malathion
Wasps	Carbaryl, pyrethrum
Winter moths on fruit trees	Chlorpyrifos

Fungicides
Most fungicides are unlikely to harm animals and birds, but many harm fish. The following chemicals are preferable to mercury-based compounds which should *not* be used.

Specific uses	Recommended treatment
Blight on potato and tomato	Copper, maneb or zineb
Bulb and corm disease	Treat before planting with quintozene dust; dip in benomyl or thiophanate-methyl
Damping-off seedlings	Copper or quintozene (as seed dressing)
Leaf spots	Benomyl, copper, maneb (roses), thiophanate-methyl or zineb
Mildews: downy	Zineb
powdery	Benomyl, copper, dinocap, sulphur, thiophanate-methyl
Moulds: on soft fruit	Benomyl, dichlofluanid, thiophanate-methyl
on vetegables and pot plants	As above. Under glass use tecnazene
Rusts	Maneb or zineb
Scabs on apples and pears	Benomyl, copper, sulphur (not sulphur-shy varieties), thiophanate-methyl
Turf diseases	Quintozene or thiophanate-methyl

Herbicides (Weedkillers)

Although most herbicides are not directly harmful to animals and birds, care should be taken when spraying, especially where gardens adjoin hedgerows. Remember that seeds and fruits of weeds like dandelions, docks, groundsel, nettles and thistles provide food for finches, so do not get rid of them unless you have to. The following products are preferred, but make sure that the one you buy is suitable for the plants you are treating.

Specific uses	Recommended treatment
Established lawns:	
Clovers	Mecoprop with 2,4-D, dicamba.
Daisy	2,4-D with mecoprop or dicamba.
Dandelion, creeping buttercup and plantains	MCPA, 2,4-D or 2,4-D mixtures.
Moss	Lawn sand based on ferrous compounds.
Variety of weeds	MCPA with dicamba or 2,4-D with dicamba or mecoprop.
Newly laid lawns	No herbicides for at least six months.
Paths, drives and tennis courts	Simazine
Vegetable gardens and flower beds, clearing weeds before planting.	Glyphosate
Prevention of germination of many annual weeds: apply to clean ground.	Propachlor granules
Problem weeds:	
Couch grass	Dalapon, used when grass is growing vigorously, but among fruit trees and bushes apply in November when tree is dormant. Glyphosate can also be used.
Bindweed, coltsfoot, dock and horsetail	MCPA, 2,4-D or 2,4-D mixtures
Dandelion	2,4-D or 2,4-D mixtures
Ground elder	Dichlobenil, when desirable plants are not close by.
Nettles	MCPA, 2,4-D or mecoprop

Slug control

The 'normal' slug killers — usually blue or green pellets — contain metaldehyde and methiocarb and are seriously harmful to wildlife and domestic pets. Accordingly they cannot be recommended or justified for use in the garden. If you do use them put them well under cover. Alternatives exist and should be sought out; the Henry Doubleday Research Association recommends, and supplies, Fertosan Slug Killer which is harmless to hedgehogs, earthworms, pets and others. Septico Slug Killer is another non-toxic control which contains aluminium sulphate, and is made in pellet form by Septico, 184 Henwood Road, Tettenhall, Wolverhampton, W. Midlands.

A simple way to trap slugs is to sink a steep-sided container in the ground to soil level and half-fill it with sweet liquid such as beer or jam and water. Remember that a hollowed out half orange or grapefruit skin placed upside down in the open will also attract them readily.

SEPTEMBER

Garden exodus

If the August garden was a quiet place for birds, September in its turn is even quieter. This month the reason is a different one; it is no longer a case of birds in deep summer moult, skulking in the depths of cover, for the moult is over and the birds are now feather perfect again. This time there is a genuine exodus of many of the resident garden dwellers for a week or two. It is almost as if, like us, they need a break from home at some time through the year. This is the season of greatest plenty in the fields and hedgerows and families of birds together with individuals both young and old, wander out into the wider countryside.

This exodus is no reflection on the supplies in your garden and in a week or two familiar birds start drifting back again leaving the hedgerows and woodland edges with their own resident birds and the arriving flocks of thrushes and finches from northern countries.

Nest boxes for the garden

September is well past the end of the breeding season for all but a few garden birds, with the exception of a few late broods of greenfinch, goldfinch, collared dove and house martin. It is a good time to look at the range of nest boxes and other artificial nest box sites which could be deployed in the garden to attract different birds to nest there. Moreover, although the next breeding season is still far away on the other side of a long dark winter, by putting up new boxes now it will give time for them to weather properly and for you to be satisfied that they are in the right positions. Just as important, it will give the garden residents the opportunity of getting used to them and sizing up possibilities; some birds may well take advantage of them for roosting in winter so that you are already building up an all-year-round population of residents.

Garden nesting birds fall readily into two main groups: those which breed in 'open' nests in hedges and bushes, and those which nest in holes. The latter group mainly comprises those which use a variety of natural holes and crevices, most frequently in broken or decaying limbs and trunks of trees. These species range from tiny birds such as blue tit and treecreeper to ones as large as stock dove and tawny owl. In an ideal world our old woodlands would contain an endless selection of hollow tree trunks and branches of different sizes. But in the heavily managed countryside of today

such sites are actually in short supply in many areas. Old woodlands have been cut down – almost half the acreage that existed at the end of the last war has since been cleared for agriculture. Furthermore new forests of soft-woods are not very attractive to most birds as they are mainly exotic conifer species and have no decaying native trees, and therefore no ready-made supply of nesting holes. To make matters worse, the Dutch elm disease which ravaged lowland elms throughout the country in the 1970s, resulted in the felling of several million trees. Elm was the most abundant lowland tree in many parts, especially on the clay lands of southern England where it was the most numerous hedgerow tree. It was also common in woodlands, spinneys and garden boundaries. Ancient elms with broken limbs, loose bark and an infinity of small holes and crannies were extremely important for most of our hole nesting birds. A number of these species have reduced in numbers since the loss of this valuable tree, almost certainly because of the resulting lack of nest sites more than consequent shortage of food.

Methods of protecting nest boxes from predation.

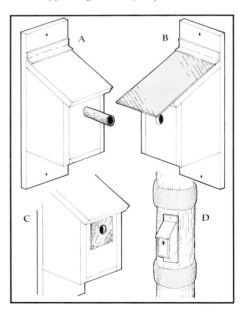

KEY

A Anti-predator tube.
B Flexible plastic roof covering.
C Metal plate around hole.
D Smooth collars around trunk.

The same situation obtains in most gardens, few of which are of sufficient size to provide ancient trees with abundant holes and hollow branches. All too often the removal of trees is one of the first steps taken when ground is cleared for building new houses. Only with luck will a few old fruit trees or other denizens escape and be a good core around which to develop a garden for birds. It takes a very long time to grow an old tree so if you can ever influence the prevention of their removal on building sites, or similar, you should do so. Thus for a variety of reasons the fact remains that hole nesting sites are usually in short supply and there is keen competition for them once spring arrives. Happily there is quite a lot the bird gardener can do to provide artificial holes and this is one area in which you can really have a positive effect on the numbers of breeding birds.

There are many woodland nest box schemes throughout the country nowadays, some of them small, some large. Such schemes have had several interesting effects. For example they have helped the spread of the attractive pied flycatchers in the western half of the country; they have greatly increased the numbers of small birds nesting in some woodland nature reserves, and have attracted new nesting species into conifer woods. Exactly the same principle applies in the garden; provide good, safe, waterproof artificial holes and you will increase the numbers and variety of birds. The total pairs nesting in garden nest boxes throughout the whole country must be enormous and like the winter feeding of birds it makes a genuine contribution to the conservation of our wild bird populations as well as providing us with endless pleasure from the opportunity it gives to watch the private lives of birds at close quarters. The following is a list of twenty-six species which might be expected to take advantage of nest boxes put up in gardens. Whether or not they turn up to do so in your particular garden depends on a whole range of factors, some of which (eg whether you are urban, suburban or rural; whether the species occurs in your part of the country) may be well beyond your control.

Garden nest box species (minimum entrance hole size is given, where applicable).

Kestrel: fairly willing to use open boxes if natural sites are missing; perhaps more likely in urban and suburban areas than rural ones.

Stock dove:
8 in (20 cm) not common in gardens unless rural and quite large.

Tawny owl:
8 in (20 cm) takes to boxes quite readily; rural or surburban.

Barn owl: less likely than formerly; decreasing; possible in artificial sites in outbuildings in rural areas.

Little owl:
4 in (10 cm) occasionally uses tawny owl or kestrel boxes: see special little owl box page 105

Swift:
5 × 3 in
(12.5 × 7.5 cm) Special nest boxes in eaves, (see page 65).

Rose-ringed parakeet:
2 in (5 cm) starling-sized box with a 2 in (5 cm) hole, if they occur in your area.

Great spotted woodpecker:
2 in (5 cm) starling size box; stuff box with wood chips or polystyrene foam nearly to entrance so that woodpecker can excavate.

House martin: special nest box (see page 49).

Pied wagtail: open fronted box well hidden in creeper etc on wall.

Grey wagtail: stream-side sites, as pied wagtail.

Wren: not a regular nest-box user; occasionally in open-fronted boxes.

Pied flycatcher:
1⅛ in (30 mm) a 'dead cert' in some rural areas in the north and west (see page 65).

Spotted flycatcher: can be persuaded into open-fronted boxes or similar, but too often has a mind of its own and plenty of natural sites to choose from.

Redstart:
1¼ in (32 mm) a classic hole nester but never the easiest to lure into boxes.

Robin: open fronted boxes, old cans, kettles etc.

Marsh tit and coal tit:
1 1/16 in (27 mm) will use boxes, but slightly reluctant tenants.

Willow tit:
1 1/16 in (27 mm) not a typical garden nester; wetter woodland; try tit box stuffed with wood chips or dead or decaying birch or alder stump; excavate their own holes.

Blue tit:
1⅛ in (30 mm) prime nest box candidate in most gardens.

Great tit:
1⅛ in (30 mm) second only to blue tit.

Nuthatch:	a ready occupant if they
$1\frac{1}{8}$ (30 cm)	occur in your garden.
Treecreeper:	see special nest box page 105.
House sparrow	an immediate snapper-up of
$1\frac{1}{4}$ in (32 mm)	any opportunity; keep out of boxes if you need to by restricting hole size to less than $1\frac{1}{4}$in (32 mm)
Tree sparrow:	willing occupants in some
$1\frac{1}{8}$ (30 mm)	areas: if one pair uses a box, put others up quickly nearby – they are colonial!
Starling:	another guaranteed first-
$1\frac{1}{2}$ in (3.75 cm)	time buyer.
Jackdaw:	nesting tunnels on trees may
6 in (15 cm)	deflect them from the house chimney if you try.

So, with a little time and trouble, some elementary carpentry, and with the necessary amount and care you can furnish the garden with a generous selection of nest box sites ready for next season. By doing so you will be of considerable help to the birds and you will enhance your own opportunities for garden bird watching either of a casual nature or more serious and investigational, whichever is your choice. At the same time you may also be able to deflect some of the problems which hole-nesting birds sometimes cause: house sparrows in air ducts, jackdaws in the chimney with a cartload of sticks, and great tits or house sparrows in the rainwater downpipes. Provide artificial sites for these species nearby and cover the problem holes with 'caps' of fine mesh galvanised netting.

There is a wide choice of nest boxes on the market nowadays and it is certainly very easy to buy the standard small-hole boxes if you wish. Many garden centres and garden shops offer a variety of refinements but be extremely wary of many of them. Not only do you need to be cautious of the materials of which they are made but also the hole size, overall dimensions and so on. It is all too easy to buy a cheap box which will either slowly barbeque nestlings when the sun shines on it in June, or one which enables a cat or squirrel to stick a paw in through the hole and scoop out the eggs or young. If you want to buy you are strongly advised to purchase from one of the dependable sources, a list of which is given on page 141.

However, many people prefer the fun of making their own nest boxes and in addition it has the advantage of being a lot cheaper. Nest boxes are basically of two different kinds: enclosed ones with small entrance holes, and others which are 'open-fronted' design, in essence nesting ledges with or without a roof. The methods of construction are similar whichever type of box you are making and several basic principles should be borne in mind. First, ensure that you use suitable timber. Buy softwood: cedar is best, but ordinary pine or deal is adequate, and it's cheaper. It should be at least $\frac{3}{4}$in (2 cm) thick, both to avoid warping and to help with temperature control at extremes of heat or cold, and should be left rough sawn (ie unplaned). As alternatives, either $\frac{1}{2}$in (1.75 cm) marine plywood (very expensive) or exterior quality plywood will do well and you can also make good use of discarded floor boards or similar second-hand planks. One is often urged that hardwood boxes of oak, beech or sycamore are best but it is dubiously justifiable to pay for such expensive wood. Properly maintained and regularly treated with wood preservative the timber we have described will last well. We have softwood boxes which have been in continual use for over twenty years and are still going strong.

Exploded view of tit box construction.

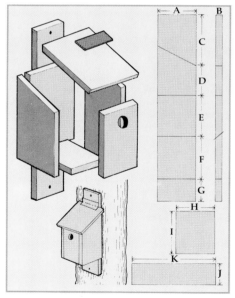

KEY

A	Width 6 in (15 cm)	**H**	Roof $8\frac{1}{2}$ in (21.5 cm)
B	Thickness $\frac{3}{4}$ in (2 cm)	**I**	Roof 10 in (25 cm)
C	Side 10 in (25 cm)	**J**	Back support (batten) 4 in (10 cm)
D	Side 8 in (20 cm)		
E	Back 10 in (25 cm)	**K**	Back support (batten) 14 in (35 cm)
F	Front 8 in (20 cm)		
G	Floor $4\frac{1}{2}$ in (11.5 cm)		

Wheatears are regular autumn migrants on downs and other open areas across the country.

Secondly you must ensure that the box is well fitted and waterproof when it is put in position. Whether the nest box has a single pitch or double pitch roof, construct it so that the roof overhangs the sides of the box and rain water thus drips off clear of the sides and also provides some shelter to the entrance hole from the worst of the rain. Use screws in the construction for preference but if you resort to nails make sure they are galvanised; you may need to replace a side or a top for one reason or another and rusted nails are likely to make it impossible to repair without splitting the wood further. If you use ordinary wire nails they will rust through in time and the box may start to open up at the joints as the timber twists. Before finally screwing your box together put a strip of sealing compound – Bostik or Seelastic – along each joint.

Some people prefer to see nest boxes looking 'more natural' and rustic than the conventional square timber homes but there is little to commend the rustic look. It certainly makes no difference whatever to the likelihood of birds occupying a box and such boxes are more difficult to make and to maintain. On balance it is probably best to give them a miss: by-pass such ones in the catalogue and don't spend your time hollowing out birch logs and the like unless that is what you particu-larly wish to have. The straightforward timber ones are quick to make, easy to maintain, accepta-ble to look at on tree, post or house wall and the birds love them.

Of the two types of basic box, the hole-type is more readily accepted than the open fronted one. Ledges and recesses in and around the garden are much easier to find than holes of the right size and many of the birds that are most numerous in our gardens are natural woodland species and hole nesters.

Making a tit box

You need an unplaned plank of timber (old floor boarding is ideal), $40\frac{1}{2}$ in $\times$ 6 in $\times \frac{3}{4}$ in (103 cm $\times$ 15 cm $\times$ 2 cm) and also one piece 10 in $\times$ 9 in (25.5 cm $\times$ 23 cm) for the roof. You also require sixteen $1\frac{1}{2}$ in screws (brass are best) or galvanised nails, a hook-and-eye or similar catch, 6 in strip of rubber, leather or thin metal sheet for the hinge and a handful of $\frac{3}{4}$ in copper tacks. The only tools you should need are a saw, plane, brace and bit (or power drill) and a screwdriver – or hammer if you are using nails.

Measure and saw the sections as shown on the construction details opposite. Use the plane to chamfer that edge of the roof piece which will be

Even little owls may be persuaded to use special nest boxes in some large gardens.

cause leaks. The hinged lid will enable you to inspect the box and clean it out easily but it is essential to use a little catch – hook-and-eye will do well – on the lid otherwise expert break-in ruffians such as squirrels or the local cat will have little difficulty in learning how to lift the lid.

Then there is the all-important question of the hole size! Almost everybody wants to know the size which will exclude house sparrows and starlings. The answer is $1\frac{1}{8}$ in (30 mm), which is the generally recommended size for tit boxes and will suit all the tits, nuthatch, wren (for winter roosting), pied flycatcher and tree sparrow. House sparrows and redstart require at least $1\frac{1}{4}$ in (32 mm) and starlings $1\frac{1}{2}$ in (28 mm). In their bigger boxes (see page 105) great spotted woodpecker and rose-ringed parakeet need 2 in (50 mm) minimum hole, pigeons need 4 in. Another important point to get right is the distance from the hole to the bottom of the tit box. This should be at least 5 in (12.5 cm) otherwise predators will be able to reach the nestlings inside. Before you drill the hole, remember to check which side (or front) you need it. It is a great pity to have made the box only to find out once you erect it in your chosen spot that you have put the hole on the wrong side and cannot see it from the window and therefore miss everything that goes on. Finally fix a 14 in × 4 in (35 cm × 10 cm) batten to the back of the box and fix through this onto the tree or wall when you erect the box. Weatherproof the box by giving it a good coat of wood preservative on the outside and both sides of the lid before you put it up. Creosote is a good dependable choice but others such as Cuprinol and other copper-based preservatives are a little more in vogue nowadays.

To make an open-fronted box use the same methods as described but leave out the hole and reduce the size of the front panel so that it gives an opening 4 in (10 cm) high in the upper half (see illustration).

Siting your tit box

Boxes can be put up at almost any height above a minimum of about 6 ft (1.8 m) and the distance above ground level is of little consequence to most of the species likely to be using them. The important thing is to make sure that it is out of reach of predators or inquisitive birds'-nesting boys. You will doubtless want to be able to look into it yourself with reasonable ease so that will determine the height too. It is quite a good idea to make a small four-rung ladder to enable you to look in the boxes when you need to.

at the back of the box so that it fits more neatly against the back panel and is easier to hinge. For the same reason chamfer the top of the front panel. Leave the back panel as the last one to be cut because the length does not need to be precise and it is immaterial if it ends up a bit longer than shown. You may have to adjust the width of the floor section a little depending on the exact thickness of your wood. Set the floor up a little way ($\frac{1}{8}$ in/3 mm or so) from the bottom of the box and drill a couple of $\frac{1}{8}$ in holes in it to assist drainage in case any water should find its way into the box. It is usually better to use a strip of leather, rubber, thin material or waterproofed canvas for the lid as conventional hinges used on top of the lid can

Avoid putting boxes in direct summer sunlight where they may heat up excessively, but at the other extreme do not hide them away in vegetation or dark north-facing corners where they will remain dreary and possibly damp. Remember too that the hole must be protected from the prevailing rainy wind so do not be afraid to tilt the box a little if necessary when you fix it. All these considerations mean that you will probably end up siting the box 6–10 ft (1.8–3 m) above the ground somewhere in the arc between north-west, through east to south-east; much however will depend on the lay-out and aspect of your individual house and garden. Try to remember that birds prefer a direct flight-line into the nest box, preferably with a perching place 6–8 ft away from the hole where they can stop and make sure the coast is clear before slipping into the box each time. So don't crowd the nest in a corner; give it a bit of space. The open-fronted 'robin' box will however be best situated where there is a bit of cover. Birds using it are much more vulnerable to attack than those safe in the fortress of a tit box, so they will be more attracted to an open one if it is well camouflaged already.

Finally one or two other do's and don'ts. Most birds like a bit of distance from their neighbours so don't put too many boxes close together (house martins and tree sparrows are exceptions). As we have seen earlier, birds will be fiercely territorial against their own kind in the breeding season although they will be less resistent to other neighbours. In general limit the number to ten or twelve boxes to the acre (football pitch size): *pro rata* in small gardens. In other words in a suburban garden 30 × 98 ft (9 × 30 m) it would certainly be worth trying a couple of tit boxes and perhaps an open-fronted box but probably no more. Don't put a nest box too close to the bird table or it will be a bit too much like living in a tent in Piccadilly and the owners will soon be stressed by the constant traffic of kerb crawlers and passers by. When you have erected your new box put a little moss or a few wood chips in the bottom. It may help attract the first settlers.

Special boxes for others

Redstarts are notoriously difficult to attract into conventional tit boxes, even in parts of the country where they are common, notably the oakwood counties of the north and west. Slightly better success was obtained on the RSPB's Gwenffrwd Reserve in Dyfed, by fixing boxes of the type shown (above) on the underside of branches. The boxes have a hole in the end which simulates a broken branch and the redstarts are a little more willing to use them.

Special nest boxes for 'other' species.

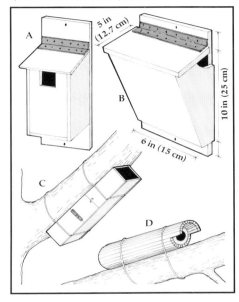

KEY
A Nest box for starlings, occasional great spotted woodpeckers and rose winged parakeets (large hole).
B Treecreeper nest box.
C Tawny owl nest box.
D Little owl nest box.

Starlings, great spotted woodpecker (occasionally) and rose-ringed parakeets will respond to bigger versions of the tit box. They need to have a depth of at least 12 in (30 cm) and an internal measurement of 5 × 5 in (12.5 × 12.5 cm) – remember that a parakeet's tail alone is 10 in (25 cm) long! You won't be able to drill out a 2 in (5 cm) diameter hole with ease but it does not have to be perfectly round so either start it off with a $\frac{3}{8}$ in drill and then use a keyhole saw, or cut the hole right at the top of the front (or side) and make it 2 in (5 cm) square.

Even bigger is the box that will be used by tawny owl, jackdaw or stock dove. Like the redstart box this should be of the 'chimney' type, resembling a broken off branch and fixed on the underside of a bough close to the bole of the tree. Because such a box is deep it may be useful to put a simple hinged flap halfway down the appropriate side panel so that you can inspect more easily. It is important that the closed end is well perforated with holes at least $\frac{1}{8}$ in in diameter so that water can drain out easily, because by its nature this box will get wet inside. This seepage can be kept to a minimum if you make the roof panel overlap and ensure that all the joints are tightly waterproof. Once you have erected it put a few handfuls of peat, sawdust or wood shavings in the bottom. Tawy owls use these boxes very readily in some areas but in other places they may show a preference for the more conventional box shape. If neither tawny owl nor stock dove use your box be assured that starlings or even robin or possibly redstart will not ignore it for long.

A nest box design for little owls was first illustrated in the *BTO News* and is shown (page 105).

Little owls do not take very readily to boxes because there is no shortage of natural sites for them. If you have them around your home it may be worth trying a box though. Site it almost on the horizontal, at 6–12 ft (2–4 m) above ground level on the underside of a branch or similar. The nest tunnel should be fairly long (at least 3 ft/1 m) and as dark as possible inside. The entrance can be as small as $2\frac{3}{4}$ in (7 cm). To see inside, make a hinged flap at the base end of the tunnel. Put sawdust or some peat in the bottom of the box.

Kestrel nest boxes have been used with success in some areas where natural sites are scarce. Although few gardens are likely to attract them to a box, if you think it worthwhile try one as follows. Make an open-fronted box approximately

Willow warblers feed intensively to build up weight before their long autumn migration.

Swallows rear successive broods through the summer, young birds still leaving the nest as late as September.

25 in × 15 in × 15 in (64 × 38 × 38 cm) with an overhang on the roof. Fix a piece of broomstick or similar along the base of the opening and project it for 1 ft (30 cm) or so as a perch. Prime the box with peat or woodshavings and site it very firmly on a high pole (20–30 ft/6–9 m), the side of the house or high on the side of a barn or stable. With the continued clearance of hedgerow trees and dying elms, natural kestrel sites are fewer than they were and you could be in luck in the right area. Tilt the box to the back a little to keep eggs and young away from the front edge. Tawny owl, stock dove or jackdaw may use the box if the kestrel doesn't.

Treecreepers are not hole nesters but instead build their nests in crevices behind loose bark, in cracks in tree trunks, in cavities behind thick ivy stems or sometimes even in wall or building crevices. One or two alternative designs can be tried for them. You can nail a length of bark longways up the trunk of a tree so that a narrow entrance is left on the side, against the tree trunk. Or you can make a special wedge-shaped treecreeper box as shown in the illustration. Whatever you do, remember the entrance must be alongside the tree trunk, but be prepared for a lack of success with these methods because the take-up is by no means guaranteed.

If you are not disposed to making any of these special boxes yourself, Jamie Wood Ltd can supply well-made woodpecker, little owl, tawny owl and kestrel boxes.

Clean out the old nest box

Do not be in too much of a hurry at the end of the breeding season to clean out the used nest box because young birds may continue to use it to roost in for some weeks after they have fledged. September is a good time to do it, so remove all the old nesting material, food remains, unhatched eggs and decaying chick carcass and burn them all on the bonfire. However clean and neat they may appear most birds are fairly heavily infested with fleas, feather mites, lice and a host of other small parasites and the old nest will harbour many of these which will hibernate there while they await the arrival of the next tenants. Once you have cleaned out the old material, dust the box lightly with a pyrethrum-based insect powder such as Cooper's Poultry Aerosol. If the box is easily removable, take it down to make a thorough job of it, and even scald it out with boiling water. Maintenance of the nest box itself involves checking the hinge and the catches, making sure that drainage holes are unblocked, and most important giving a seasonal coat of creosote or cuprinol if it is needed, to ensure that the box remains waterproof. When the nest box is back in place and clean, put some dry moss, shavings or a few grasses and leaves in it because it may well be used as a winter roost.

Swift nest boxes are something of a special case. Because they are tucked safely into the roof space they need no normal maintenance and it is best to leave the nest platform intact in the nest. However swifts are more heavily infested with parasites than any other home-and-garden bird and the boxes should be given a good dose of insecticide in September, when the birds have long since gone.

Departing summer visitors

By September there are few of the ever-welcome summer visitors still remaining in the gardens. Cuckoos departed two months ago, soon followed by the swifts and after them the warblers, flycatchers, redstarts and turtle doves. Now only the rearguard of the summer batallions is still here. Among the gathering parties of tits, goldcrests and others, individual willow warblers and chiffchaffs still linger although there is little to tell whether they are the remnants of the season's local population or a constantly changing company of birds which are passing through from further north. Chiffchaffs in particular are notable for the fact that they sing regularly in autumn, even if the song evidently lacks the urgency and fresh-

ness of spring. Feeding is good for them among the legions of midges, gnats and aphids on the leaves of sallows, willows and birches and they sing to maintain a movable feeding territory around them as they travel south.

However, the main cohorts of the summer rearguard are the swallows and martins. Still feeding youngsters from third broods of the season they continue to flourish on the bounty of small flying insects in the warm Indian-summer days of September. But they are gathering now in increasing numbers as each day passes. They line the telephone wires in uneasy gatherings, agitated and restless and skim in loose companies low over the fields on the damp heavy days, or sweep lazy and relaxed above the houses and gardens on the warmer and breezy days. They make sudden mass excursions from the wires and sometimes rise high in the sky calling excitedly so that we think they are surely parting, but they settle again and are still there the next day. All too soon however they will be gone, leaving only a handful of the latest breeders to catch them up in the days that follow. They have momentous journeys to make. The house martins will head for West Central Africa but the swallows are bound much further, to the

Berry bearing plants.

KEY
A Ivy (*Hedera helix*)
B Cotoneaster
C Firethorn (*Pyracantha atlantioides*)
D Hawthorn

high veldt and sunshine of South Africa, an awesome journey of some 6000 miles and one on which many of their numbers will succumb. Both swallows and martins are daytime migrants so are able to hunt *en route*, unlike those migrants which fly at night and are forced to make lengthy daytime stops to restock with food. The swallows long pointed wings are well designed for powerful long distance flight, similar in that respect to falcons, swifts, bee-eaters and many shore birds, and these wings will carry the swallows southwards at a steady speed of about thirty-seven miles per hour, some seven to eight miles per hour faster than their 'normal' level flight. Swallows arrive with us well before their breeding season begins and leave relatively late; swifts return in May and have gone immediately their young are on the wing by the end of July and yet both birds have very similar feeding needs and habits. The wide difference between them in this respect remains yet another of the unknown mysteries of the bird world.

September wagtails

Lawns are important feeding places as we have already seen. Not only are they full of juicy nutritious worms but they are also alive with myriad tiny midges and flies. The pied wagtail is a good example of a garden bird which takes full advantage of this feeding, and September is the very best wagtail month. They are amongst the most active and energetic of ground feeders, rushing after flies and other small insects across the short turf and dancing into the air to pursue selected morsels. When searching the lawn they strut purposefully, looking all around them, their long tails constantly flicking.

September is their particular month because at this time both adult birds and the season's youngsters are heading southwards all across the country in a gentle rolling wave of migration. Their migration is one of the easiest to see because of their fondness of feeding on closely mown lawns and playing fields. Notice, on the local playing fields or school lawns, how the numbers change each day, how they build up in September and then drop off again as the rolling tide slowly passes by. Bird books rightly tell you that the pied wagtail is a resident bird but it is only a small proportion which remains for the winter while the great majority pass south to France and Spain. On the coasts of Sussex, Kent or Devon huge numbers strike out to sea from the headlands in September and early October.

The individuals which remain in winter will continue to visit your lawn. As the insect crop dies off they will be grateful for the tiny unconsidered crumbs which others leave below the bird table. Elsewhere, like so many other winter residents — blackbird, robin, mistle thrush, marsh tit — the wagtails will each defend their own waterside food supply, establishing a territory of precisely the right size to assure their needs for the winter and patrolling it as regularly as a sentry throughout the daylight hours.

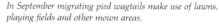

In September migrating pied wagtails make use of lawns, playing fields and other mown areas.

*September sees the departure of most of our summer
visitors; swallows gather on the wires in numbers and once
they do this they will not be with us much longer.*

OCTOBER

Members of the thrush family are foremost of those attracted to berry crops.

October sees the garden hedges and shrubs full with berries and fruits and is the perfect time to assess just how productive the garden is in this respect and decide whether or not there is more that can easily be provided. Late autumn is also one of the best times of year to establish new shrubs. It is also the time for clearing and tidying flower borders and deciding whether there are further plants which you can establish here that will be beneficial to birds and other wildlife in the garden.

Berries for birds

One of the advantages of berry-bearing shrubs is that there is such a wide choice available nowadays that it is easy to find ones to suit your particular needs in relation to aspect, size, spread etc. Suggestions such as those made here involve plants which are well known to be favourites with birds, but the list is nowhere near comprehensive and your nurseryman will be able to give you the local advice you need on suitability to your soil type, availability, growing form and ultimate size. Many varieties can be trained against walls and

fences thus taking up less space but still producing heavy berry crops – and often providing nesting or roosting sites as well. Make maximum use of your wall spaces in this respect.

There is a great range of berry bearing shrubs which are attractive to birds and other garden wildlife and many of them have dense flowers which are not only welcome additions to the colours of the garden but are also beloved by insects and therefore doubly useful to birds. Four major families of shrubs can between them provide the bulk of the selection from which the bird gardener may well decide to choose:

Pyracanthas	**(Firethorns)**
Berberis	**(Barberry)**
Cotoneasters	
Honeysuckles	

Pyracantha In addition to the merits of a huge berry crop, the great attribute of the evergreen firethorns is their willingness to grow uninhibited in totally sunless or north facing sites and still produce masses of white blossom and later a harvest of fruit. One of the best known varieties *Pyracantha crenulata*, 'Orange Glow', is named after the prolific mass of orange berries. Other good varieties are *Pyracantha atlantoides*, an upright fast-growing plant, with bright red fruit and *P. rogersian*, variety 'Flava', with yellow berries. *P. angustifolia* has the usual hawthorn-like flowers in flat umbels and bright orange-yellow berries. None of the pyracanthas are climbers and they need a degree of tying or training to keep them reasonably flat to the wall. Excellent for nest sites. All these varieties produce heavy crops of fruit in autumn which are well used by birds.

Berberis This is an enormous family of shrubs with some 450 species and a wide range of varieties on offer in garden centres. There are both deciduous and evergreen varieties, the latter being useful as early-season nest sites for thrushes and blackbirds although the deciduous varieties tend to be the heaviest berry bearers. Several of the species make good hedging plants, eg *Berberis thunbergii*. Other popular varieties are *B. darwinii* which has dark glossy evergreen leaves, rich yellow flowers, and purple berries, *B. wilsoniae* which is deciduous and a particularly heavy fruiter. *B. bookeri* is deciduous with holly-like leaves, clusters of yellow flowers and black ovoid berries and *B. aggregata* also bears bright panicles of yellow flowers and has attractive waxy coral-red berries.

Cotoneaster A family of some fifty evergreen and deciduous species ranging from small prostrate mat-forming types to tall free-standing bushes. *Cotoneaster horizontalis* is the best-known variety, admired for its flat herring-bone growing form and the willingness with which it clothes fences and walls (but may need tying in) including north-facing ones. Its masses of scarlet berries are much favoured by birds – waxwings love them. Also try *C. bullatus* which is deciduous but fruits over a long period, *C. conspicuus* with a mound of dense arching stems, masses of white flowers and large fruit, or the semi-evergreen hybrid *C. cornubia* whose autumn branches are borne down by the weight of the big red fruit. *C. microphyllus* is an extremely robust low-growing shrub particularly useful for covering bare ground, banks or unsightly ground. It has a heavy crop of scarlet berries. *C. dammeri* and *C. prostrata* are also ground-hugging, ever-spreading trailers which give good ground cover. *C. aldenhamensis* and *C. waterari* grow slowly into small trees.

Honeysuckle There are over 200 known honeysuckles so choice is again wide and your main concerns will probably be the visual appearance of the flowers (different varieties have coloured stems and interesting leaves) and the number of succulent berries they will yield. Of the hardy species the native woodbine *Lonicera periclymenum* is too well known to need description. *L. japonica* has an unforgettable fragrance and rapid growth. *L. tellmanniana* has scentless flowers on a mass of yellow blossom and will grow happily in full shade. All these varieties should produce good berry crops.

Apart from these four main families a number of other hardy shrubs are well worth including in the garden if you can fit them in. The naturalised snowberry produces pulpy marble-sized white berries, and dogwood (various forms) which is often grown for its attractive red winter stems has attractive umbels of flowers and black berries. *Daphne* is a rare native plant but very common in its garden forms; its tight stem-hugging clusters of scarlet berries are taken by thrushes and are special favourites with greenfinches. The big quince-like fruits of *japonica* remain on the bush until well through the winter and thrushes will then take them when other foods are scarce. Other berry bearing shrubs worth considering include *skimmia*, *Garrya* (requires male and female plants), purging buckthorn, *Callicarpa* (*C. japonica luxurians* has the largest berry clusters) and of course blackberries of various species. One early-fruiting shrub which blackbirds and some warblers cannot resist is the Oregon grape *Mahonia aquifolium*. It is a suckering shrub with dark green leathery leaves which flowers early, in March and April, producing rich fragrant yellow flowers which are followed by tight bunches of blue-black berries in August and September.

A final word should be said about an indispensable shrub, buddleia, although it is not berry-bearing and does not attract birds directly. It is often referred to as the 'butterfly bush' because of its infallible attraction to butterflies, moths and other late summer insects. No garden should be without at least one buddleia and they come in many glowing forms and shades.

The bird table

October is still a month of plenty but nonetheless it is the time to start organising the provision of food for the winter and making sure you have all the right feeding facilities needed for your individual garden. The traditional way of feeding, other than by putting food scraps on the ground, is with a bird table and although it may have some limitations and shortcomings it is still the most satisfactory basic method. There is an increasing variety of other ideas for bird feeding devices and these are looked at in the November chapter, but the common element to most garden feeding stations is some form of bird table. It may be that you are lucky and have a ready-made table in the form of an old tree stump, wall top or similar, but usually it is necessary to provide a purpose-made bird table.

Basically your table can be supported either on a post or wall bracket, or can be free hanging from a tree branch or similar. Your own requirements and circumstances will determine which method you use as there is little to choose between them so long as you understand the one or two essential requirements for birds — and so long as you keep the 'cat problem' ever in mind. The table should not be put where it is surrounded by close cover as many species will be justly nervous of using it there for fear of being surprised by predators. At the same time try to avoid putting it *too* far from cover as the birds may then feel over exposed to predators; notice how many of the birds like to approach in cautious stages, moving from one perch to another rather than flying a good way across a wide open lawn. Nearby perches also make it easier for them to stay close by when they have been ejected by birds higher up the peck order. You can put your table as close to the house as you like, but it is worth remembering that movements inside the windows will constantly frighten off the feeding birds and some of the shier species will be very reluctant to use it (although you may see this as an advantage with starlings and house sparrows!).

Whether your table is hanging or on a post, it is best situated 5–6 ft (1.5–2 m) above the ground. If you use a post, a galvanised metal one is best as it

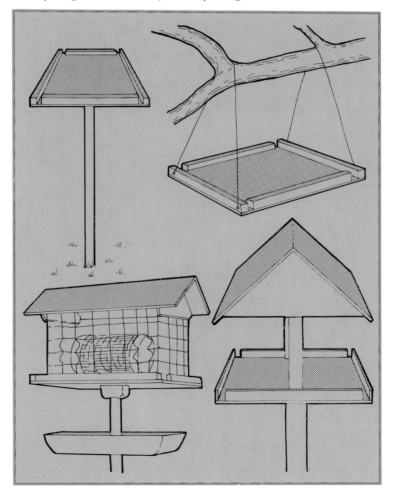

Different bird table models. (Bottom left- the Sussex bird table)

deters cats and grey squirrels from climbing to the table. The simpler the table the better. You may find that bird tables which incorporate a water bowl cause problems when birds drink or bathe too enthusiastically and drench the food. The feeding tray should be between 2–4 sq ft. (30–60 sq cm) and should have a coaming around it to prevent the food being blown or knocked off the table. A gap or two in the coaming facilitates cleaning and allows rainwater to run off. Although it is not essential, a roof is a very good idea as it helps to keep the food dry and is often used by the customers to shelter from a heavy shower. A roof can also be used to fit in a seed hopper or other device where it is necessary to keep the food items (seed etc) dry.

As with the tit box, you can either decide to buy your bird table ready made, or you can make it yourself. The RSPB produces a very good DIY leaflet which tells you everything you need to know, should you decide to make your own. The RSPB's DIY instructions are set out below.

'Use a piece of exterior quality plywood or similar board which will not split in wet weather, about 12 × 20 in (30 × 50 cm) in size and $\frac{1}{2}$ in to $\frac{3}{4}$ in (1 cm to 2 cm) thick. Fit some strips of wood about 1 cm high along each side to form a rim around the edge but leave a gap at each corner to make it easier to sweep clean and to let water drain out. The strips can be screwed on from beneath, which is less likely to split the wood than using nails.

To hang a table, use small screw-in eyes or hooks at each corner. Attach equal lengths of nylon cord or light metal chain to each hook and tie together in the centre, or, better still, make a loop at either end across a horizontal branch; this stops the table from spinning round.

If you fix it to a post, use one 5–6 ft (150–200 cm) long and make it firm in the ground. Metal is best but wood is easier to fit to the table. Use some plastic piping to cover a wooden post in order to stop cats and squirrels climbing to the table. Fix a wooden post to the table by using metal right-angle brackets.

A few nails or hooks in the edges of the table will be useful for hanging nut bags or wire baskets for kitchen scraps. Lumps of fat, fatty bones or peanuts in shells can all be hung on a string from one of these hooks.

Once it is constructed treat the whole table with wood preservative. Creosote is fine if it is allowed to dry thoroughly before the table is erected but otherwise use Cuprinol or one of the other copper based wood preservatives'.

The garden robin – popular and confiding.

However, if you are inclined to buy your bird table there are several very reliable makes on the market from which you can choose. The RSPB can sell you a basic but excellent roofed table with or without seed hopper and also a more comprehensive 'Bird Haven' table which incorporates a water bowl, nut tower and unclimbable PVC-coated steel post. A smaller model, also roofed, is the 'Bird House Feeder' made of firm polypropylene with a central nut column and individual compartments in the 13 in (32.5 cm) circular table for different food items; it fits neatly onto a broom handle as a post. Jamie Wood Ltd produce a basic roofed table (no seed hopper) which is strongly constructed and they also have a smaller hanging version marketed as a feeding tray. In a higher price range Jamie Wood can offer the novel Sussex Bird Table which is a double-decker feeder (see illustration). The top storey is proofed against starlings, squirrels and other larger intruders while admitting all the tits and nuthatch, robin and other small birds. It looks a little elaborate but in fact is a good idea and works very well (the horizontal nut feeder is a bit close to the surface of the table and restricts the available feeding area unnecessarily). A spring-loaded wire door permits easy re-stocking. The lower deck is a durable plastic tray (14 × 10 in/35 × 25 cm) with good 2 in (5 cm) sides and it is supplied with a rustproof aluminium pole. This interesting table is a handsome and user-friendly addition to the bird garden even if each of its separate functions can be achieved more cheaply by a combination of individual feeding devices.

Pippaware supply a good plastic bird table on a sectional metal pole. It is 13 in (34 cm) in diameter and has a built-in drinking bath. It is easy to clean and erect, with a good spike on the bottom section of the pole to stick in the lawn.

Various other firms including Nerine Nurseries, Scottish National Institution for the War Blinded and Scandinavian Design also make good bird tables (and often other garden bird furniture too) and it is advisable to stick to one or more of these reputable suppliers. Many garden centres and the like now supply bird tables but you should be cautious of them; do not be persuaded by 'natural look' or pseudo rustic versions as they are often non-durable, especially when made of birch which looks attractive initially but soon becomes dilapidated. Avoid elaborate gnome-encrusted or ornate 'designer' bird tables, especially those which have grotesque 'natural' poles and limbs which are nothing more than inviting adventure playgrounds for cats and squirrels. It is probably best to shun multi-functional edifices too, such as those containing nest boxes in the roof as no self-respecting bird wishes to nest in the middle of a bird table used by all and sundry.

Try to avoid siting the bird table in full sunlight or in deep shade and remember that wind is one of the most annoying hazards, either stockpiling all the goodies at one end (always the wet end!) or blowing them onto the ground. Bird tables get dirty very quickly so ensure that stale and rotten food is removed and that the table is cleaned regularly. Scrub with boiling water every now and then. A properly sited and well-run bird table will be the focal point of all bird activity in the garden, certainly through the winter half of the year, so be prepared to spend time and make sure it is right.

Taming garden birds

It is one of the small summits of achievement and trust for some dedicated bird gardeners to encourage sufficient confidence in a garden bird that it will come to feed from the hand or will enter the house for daily rations. There is no reason why anyone should not do this if they wish, given the strong proviso that by so doing they do not put the birds in jeopardy. It is unwise and unfair to tame robin, chaffinch, great tit or others if there is any risk that their confidence and tameness will result in them being snatched by the cat or being scared by the bouncing poodle or rampaging children into crashing into windows when they have been tempted into the kitchen for morsels.

Take a lot of time and show plenty of patience. Tempt your target bird closer and closer over a period of days (or weeks) by throwing favourite scraps closer and closer to you, or drawing the

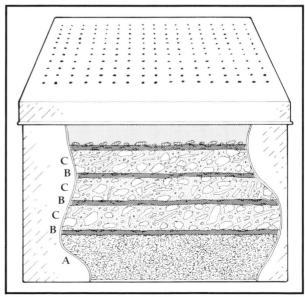

Meal worm factory.

KEY
A Dried bran or barley
B Hessian sacking
C Layer of vegetables

The colourful but enigmatic bullfinch is a silent and cautious visitor to the garden.

items of food closer to the back door or the open window all the time. In the end patience will reward you and the robin, blue tit or great tit will accept the food from your open hand (but keep stock-still) or the kitchen table. Robins are possibly the most readily confiding and will make a welcome daily kitchen visitor. Pick your species with care however: feel for Joyce Ablitt at Aberdyfi, whose kindness was rewarded by the increasing tameness of a local herring gull who thinks nothing of marching into the living room and calling for food when it is not liberally supplied on the balcony. Pretty large and potentially messy things herring gulls, especially when walking into the house whenever door or window is left open.

Know the sorts of food items which each species is likely to find most irresistable. Robins, for example, will sell their souls for a beakful of juicy, wriggling mealworms!

Mealworm culture

You can buy mealworms from any good pet shop but buying becomes an expensive business if you want to keep a ready supply for the bird table. It is a relatively simple process to grow your own, and costs very little. Live mealworms are nutritious and irresistable bird-table food, loved by robins, blackbirds and most other visitors with the obvious exception of the seed eaters. The mealworm is the larva of a common brown beetle

(*Tenebrio molitor*) which is a pest in granaries and cereal stores. It is extensively bred for its larvae to supply the pet trade as a food for 'soft bill' birds, lizards etc. Do not confuse these mealworms with 'gentles' which are also sold as fishing bait in angling shops; these maggots are the larvae of 'blowflies' and although birds love them they are smelly and pretty unsavoury creatures to keep in the house.

To grow your own mealworms, find a fairly large container – old biscuit tin, crock or goldfish bowl – and clean it well. If it has smooth slippery sides so much the better as it will help to contain the little grubs which can climb with surprising skill. Put 1–2 in (3–5 cm) of wheat bran, rolled oats or flour in the bottom. Cover it with a layer of hessian and then a layer of raw potato, cabbage, carrot, banana or apple skins as may be available; add one or two slices of dry, stale bread. Repeat the layers two or three times until your mealworm factory is filled to within a few inches of the top. Make sure that your fruit and veg layer is not too wet and juicy or the mixture will ferment and rot, and not only smell appalling but will kill the mealworms too. A good mixture should not smell. Introduce 200–300 live mealworms (and/or a few beetles if you want to speed up the crop of successive generations). The mealworms will change into creamy-white pupae in a week or two from which the adult beetles will emerge a few weeks later. They will lay more eggs which grow into

117

Fieldfares and redwings are large-scale autumn immigrants from Scandinavia.

little fat mealworms and represent your first crop. As you take them to feed to the birds remember the principles of conservation and ensure that you are only cropping the surplus and leaving an adequate breeding stock.

In a few weeks your mealworm factory will be reduced to a dry dusty powder and you need to renew the food layers. If you wish to expand your production, simply build more biscuit-tin factories; move one of the pieces of dry bread into each one as it will contain plenty of eggs. Keep the breeding colonies somewhere warm – the airing cupboard is ideal – and the beetles will perform best at a constant temperature of around 75°F (25°C). The cooler it is the slower they will breed. No lid is needed on the containers except to prevent escapes although other expedients may make it sensible to use one. A perforated lid or piece of butter muslin will suffice and plenty of air must circulate. When you need to gather your mealworm crop fold a sheet of paper into a concertina and put it in the jar overnight. The mealworms will collect in the folds and be easy to gather when you carefully lift the paper out. Otherwise you need to sieve them from the top layer of bran. An adult beetle lives for ten weeks and each female lays 500–700 eggs which take just over a week to hatch; the mealworms then stay in a larval stage

for several months before pupating. Start your mealworm city in October and you will be ready for the winter.

A gentle word of warning: mealworm culture sounds easy but it does need to be done with care and attention. If you don't succeed you may have to resort to buying and in this event the following mealworm stockists will be happy to oblige if you cannot find any locally.

Farmers Factory, 8 Broadway, Mill Road, Cambridge CB1 3AH

Ponderosa Avaries, White House, Branch House, The Reddings, Cheltenham GL51 6RP

Phoenix Birdfood Ltd, St Lukes Church Hall, Shireoak, Worksop, Notts S81 8LX

EW Coombs Ltd, 25 Frinsbury Road, Strood, Kent.

The flower border

A garden which is full of flowering plants through spring and summer will certainly be alive with insects too. More insects mean more food for a variety of birds so that all the insect-attracting garden flowers are to be encouraged. The list of good insect plants is very long but includes lavenders, hebe, iceplant, sweet rocket, rosemary, michaelmas daisy, aster, alyssum, cosmos, evening primrose, petunia, valerian, thyme, primrose, clarkia, godetia.

Birds as varied as warblers, tits, goldcrest and spotted flycatcher will profit from the insects attracted to these flowers. Goldfinches will take the seeds of poppies, michaelmas daisy, aster, cornflower and even golden rod and alyssum as well as their favourite teasel. Bullfinches will sample the wallflower and snapdragon seeds if times are hard and greenfinch, house sparrows and various tits will thank you if you find room for sunflowers and leave the heavy heads in place to seed. The massive, giant hogweed – up to 15 ft (3 m) tall at times – is a rather awesome plant, being both highly invasive from its seed and capable of producing a nasty skin rash through its juice. If you dare try it – it is best in a damp spot – its white table-top flowerheads are packed with insects and the whole plant is much used by feeding warblers, tits, goldcrest and flycatchers.

Autumn arrivals – thrushes and the bachelor bird

The British garden chaffinch is a complete stay-at-home and will probably not move more than a few hundred yards from home the whole of its life. Ringing recoveries show that even young birds seldom move more than 3 miles (5 km) from their natal area to set up their own territories and usually it is much less than that. So the probability is that the chaffinches on your lawn in autumn and winter are exactly the same individuals – and their offspring – that were there in spring and summer.

However, this is only half the chaffinch story because in October and November there is a vast exodus of chaffinches from Scandinavia and other areas around the Baltic Sea as they migrate south and west to the snow-free fields of Britain. They move through Denmark, Holland and Belgium in huge flocks and then turn west to make the short sea-crossing to south-east England before fanning out again all over the country. The hen birds travel in advance of the cocks which arrive a few days later and then remain in their bachelor parties all throughout the winter. It is these massed tides of chaffinches which form single-sex flocks feeding in arable fields of lowland Britain for they do not mix at all with our native residents. These two wholly separate populations of chaffinches live side by side through the British winter. Look at these flocks and you will probably find that most comprise male birds because a lot of the female flocks pass further west from the peninsulas of Wales to the even milder fields of Ireland.

Stand in the garden on a quiet still night in October and listen for some of the other vikings

In late summer goldfinches are likely to visit gardens to feed on thistle heads and the seeds of other late summer garden plants.

Long-tailed tits are delicate and acrobatic birds feeding on
tiny insects in leaf axils and among clusters of berries or
buds.

Scrap feeding basket.

which are now arriving. Wherever your garden is, north or south, town or country, you will not have long to wait before you hear the soft, faint *seeep* of redwings passing overhead in the dark. As you hear successive calls from left and right you will build up a picture of an endless stream of loose batallions of thrushes moving south and west across the whole breadth of the country. Listen carefully and try to distinguish the *seeep* of the redwings from the near identical but slightly shorter *tsip* of the song thrushes. These are the contact calls which keep the birds in touch with their neighbours as they drive on unseen through the night sky. A small proportion of the redwings and fieldfares (but probably none of the northern song thrushes) will remain here for the winter and become the familiar flocks foraging in the fields and hedgerows, later to visit the garden in hard weather looking for apples and other wasted fruit. The majority will pass straight on to France, Iberia and Ireland.

Huge numbers of blackbirds from Europe also arrive at this time of year and many of them will remain in Britain for the winter. The exodus from the Continent will bring others to the garden too, bramblings in flocks to feed on beech mast, sometimes mainland great tits and blue tits escaping the continental cold and with luck a party of colourful waxwings to feed confidingly on the cotoneaster and berberis berries on the house walls.

The last house martins

Improbable though it seems, the last pairs of house martins may yet have youngsters in their mud nests tucked up high under the eaves of the house. In many years, especially in the south of England, young from third broods are still in the nest in the first half of the month. The adult birds are tired and jaded by now and their plumage has lost its bright blue hue as summer passed and they became browner and more worn. Some of the young birds from earlier broods still await departure with the adults, but for them the waiting time is an important learning period too. In the shortening days of summer it was they who were responsible for the new outlines of nesting cups etched in gobbets of mud alongside the 'real' nests; these apprentices' nests are their training for the real thing next year. Now, as the harvest of flying insects gets smaller these same youngsters help the adults, and add to their own experience, by bringing in insects and taking part in the feeding of the nestlings. Watch the birds as they go to the nest and you will see the adults in their worn and duller colours, and the young birds, brighter and bluer.

121

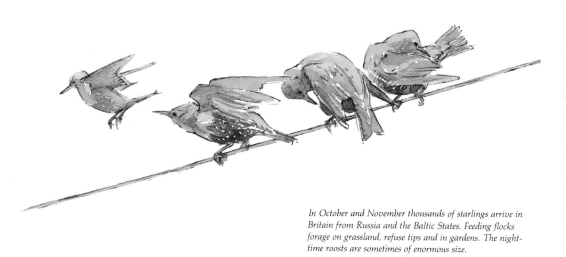

In October and November thousands of starlings arrive in Britain from Russia and the Baltic States. Feeding flocks forage on grassland, refuse tips and in gardens. The night-time roosts are sometimes of enormous size.

NOVEMBER

Winter feeding

November is the time to start the winter feeding in earnest, to habituate the garden birds to the food supply and to ensure that you have got your season's stock of peanuts, seed and other supplies assured. With your bird table newly made or the old one well cleaned and scrubbed, you may well want to add other feeding devices to attract more specialist feeders or to bring birds close up to your window. The range of foods which can be offered to birds is very wide. You can make a great deal yourself if you have the time and inclination, but if your life is busy and your pocket can stand it, you can buy an ever-increasing range of good garden bird foods which will provide adequately for the needs of many species, but can never rival the diversity you can provide by taking a little more time and trouble. The two critical elements are to feed the right foods and feed regularly once you start. If you go away for a winter holiday it is just as important to have a neighbour put out your bird food daily as it is for him to feed the cat. Once you start feeding birds you really must continue with daily regularity through the winter. If you cut off their supply in hard weather you are very likely to condemn them to early starvation because they have learned to rely heavily on your feeding station: without it they would otherwise have established a completely different foraging pattern which allowed for alternatives if one of their main sources of food failed, so now you cannot let them down.

Feed at the most important times of day too, early morning and mid-afternoon, which coincide with the main feeding periods before and after roosting when birds have the greatest need to build up their resources. Remember too that it is important to put food in the right places: some birds feed only on the ground (dunnock, yellowhammer, pied wagtail) while others prefer a table, and some are best catered for by hanging feeders (tits, nuthatch, woodpeckers). Most of our bird table species are more at ease feeding at a reasonable distance from the house and the shier species such as woodpecker, tree sparrow and reed bunting may be penalised when their needs are greatest if the food is put too close to your house.

When you provide food for the ground feeders it is a good idea to place it on a simple tray so that it can then be taken in at night and not serve to attract rats and mice. Rats in particular should be discouraged at all costs; in addition to their other objections they are frequent carriers of *salmonella* which can easily spread to birds and may cause serious mortality. For these sorts of reasons it is also a good idea to move the ground feeding station once or twice a winter if you are able.

What foods to offer

Different species of birds eat completely different foods. Thus by putting stale bread on the lawn you will satisfy the local starlings, sparrows and street pigeons but will offer nothing to a nuthatch or a great tit. Conversely a peanut feeder will sustain a blue tit, greenfinch or nuthatch through the deepest cold spell but leave the blackbirds and robins starving. The art of feeding garden birds lies in providing an epicurean self-service buffet catering for the tastes of vegetarian, carnivore, seed-eater and insectivore. As winter encroaches all birds have need for foods which are rich in carbohydrates to help them build up rapid reserves of body fat for the long cold nights. Therefore items with a high fat content are particularly important: suet, bone marrow, dripping, peanuts, cheese, bacon rind, sun-flower seed.

Kitchen scraps and the scrap basket

The range of suitable kitchen scraps which can be fed to the birds is almost limitless. Steer clear of slushy meal remains and cooked vegetables which are messy and unlikely to be eaten, but otherwise make good use of such items as stale cake, broken biscuits, dry cheese (the 'blue' varieties and strongly flavoured ones will tend to be left), pastry (cooked or uncooked), cooked (especially baked) potatoes, currants, sultanas, dried peas, lentils, cooked rice, bacon rinds, meat bones, sponge pudding, oats or oatmeal and bread. Bread is rightly condemned as being among the least nutritious of foods we can put out for birds. Wholemeal bread is certainly better than 'cotton-wool' white but no bread is actually harmful; it is simply that on its own it is insufficient to provide a balanced bird diet. So do not hesitate to use it, especially where fat-rich foods and other choices are also on offer. Despite its advertised disadvantages white bread has a calcium content which is helpful in maintaining feather, beak and claw condition. Break it up into small crumbs and if it is very stale and hard soak it first. As mentioned elsewhere bread can be used to advantage in trying to deflect the starling hoards from more valuable offerings.

Experiment with different kitchen foods and you will soon discover which the birds prefer and which they will spurn. There are no hard and fast rules for kitchen scraps, just common sense and experiment.

Some of the scraps you should put on the bird table and some on the ground feeder. A good hanging scrap basket is a very useful idea and has the obvious advantage of stopping the scraps being blown about and scattered on the ground below. By far the best types are the stout wire hanging baskets, plastic covered and with a fitting lid; they are easy to fill and to clean and prevent wholesale thieving through the top. The RSPB makes a good one which is very reasonably priced and other firms also have a variety of similar models. It is well worth the modest expense of a scrap basket if your only other alternative is a nylon mesh peanut bag or similar which very quickly becomes messy. When buying a basket avoid any model which is made of collapsible wire mesh as there is a constant danger of birds becoming trapped by leg or foot between the separate wire sections.

Nuts

Nuts are good and popular bird food. Any type of nut will do the job so it is worth shelling any that have been left over from last Christmas and putting them out; wedge a few in crevices in posts or tree trunks for the nuthatches and woodpeckers while you are at it. Hazel nuts can be gathered in autumn if you have the time and can get there before the squirrels, and stale kitchen walnuts or shelled almonds are always welcome. The great standby however is peanuts – a bird food *par excellence*! Buy them shelled and in bulk from reputable bird food firms or pay twice as much for the pre-packed versions in mesh bags ready for hanging – but remember that it is in red mesh bags that siskins are particularly attracted to peanuts in late winter. Don't underestimate the amount of peanuts the birds may get through in the course of a winter. If you think in terms of 3lb or so per week you may be somewhere near the mark, so think in bulk and order early because it is in a good cause! There are various ways in which to offer peanuts but if you put them loose on the bird table they will disappear at an amazing rate. As well as being devoured on the spot, visitors such as coal tit and nuthatch will ferry them away wholesale to hide for another time. The best way to present them is in one of the many nut feeders now on the market. Once again be cautious in your buying and go to reputable suppliers. Avoid any with sharp edges, or those made of a tapering wire spiral which end in a point and make a deadly leg trap. The RSPB

Tits will be the first birds to visit hanging strings of peanuts; other species, such as chaffinch, can only watch and wait for fallen scraps.

offers one or two sound types of nut feeder (see illustrations on page 133 later in this section) as do some of the other firms selling bird garden equipment (see page 141).

Blue tits, great tits and coal tits will be the first to find the hanging peanut feast but they will soon be joined by nuthatch, greenfinch and even house sparrow. Squirrels will try their luck and so may unlikely species such as dunnock, robin, reed bunting and blackcap, to say nothing of the resourceful great spotted woodpecker and the starling. There are ways and means of excluding the larger of these visitors if you wish to and if the nuts are going at too fast a rate. The Sussex bird table

Some birds, for example yellowhammer, feed only on the ground.

(page 114) is one method and there are innumerable similar devices on the market. It is also fairly easy to devise your own exclusion methods as Mr Piggott from Easington in North Humberside did. He cut the base off a plastic bottle and drilled a hole through its cap, and then hung the nut feeder inside the sawn-off bottle with a wire threaded through the cap to hang on the original branch again. If the bottle is cut exactly the right length the tits feed happily from the base of the feeder while the less agile species are defeated and can do little more than wait on the ground for fallen morsels.

If you have some salted peanuts left over from a party there is no reason why you cannot use these as the amount of salt on them is unlikely to be harmful to birds. The RSPB recommends however that they should be well washed and then thoroughly dried in the oven before being put out. The RSPB also advises that you should beware of using dirty or mouldy peanuts which smell musty as they can develop a powerful poison – aflatoxin – which kills liver cells and has caused the death of many garden birds. Do not buy such nuts, but at the same time do not confuse them with broken or wrinkled nuts which may be unattractive but perfectly acceptable to birds.

Some people prefer to provide peanuts in the shell, strung together and hung from a branch or wall bracket. This is fine but if you do it, take note of the risk of birds' legs and feet becoming entangled in fine cotton or string. It is much better to use smooth thick plastic line or to skewer the nuts on a length of galvanised wire. Cut one end of the wire on the slant to make a point and bend it over once the wire is full to prevent the nuts falling off. Bend the top end into a hook to suspend it. If you attach it to its fixing point with an elastic band or similar it will spin round and round as the tits settle on it to extract the peanuts and they seem to enjoy the twirling carousel it produces.

Before peanuts are manufactured into human foods (peanut butter, peanut bars etc) each nut is split and the tiny peanut germ – the growing point of the new plant – is removed because it has a slightly bitter taste. Bitter it may be to the human palate, but we know that to birds it is the peak of gastronomic perfection. Supplies of this peanut germ are now marketed by one firm, CJ Wildbird Foods Ltd (address on page 141), with the well justified claim that even those garden birds which do not normally take peanuts, find these peanut germs completely irresistible. Provide them either in standard dispensers or on the bird table but also scatter some on the ground for those species which only feed at ground level. If there is one food item which will bring in new species to the garden it is this peanut germ. One word of warning however; do not overfeed birds on it, make sure they have what they need but do not provide them with a surplus.

Coconuts are well liked, especially by the tit family, nuthatches and woodpeckers. The ideal way to present them is by sawing them in half and hanging upside down through a hole drilled in the end. Re-use the empty shells to put special 'bird cake' in (see recipe on page 128). Whereas whole coconut is a splendid bird food, on no account feed birds with dessicated coconut which expands severely when moistened – as when inside a bird's stomach.

Fats

Suet is probably the simplest and most rewarding way of providing fat at the bird table. Either tie it up to a branch or a hook on the bird table, or skewer it on a piece of wire. If the friable pieces are too small use them in the scrap basket. However, fat comes in a wide variety of other forms too and it is so important to birds in winter that it should never be allowed to go to waste. Bacon rinds can be hung up on a string or cut in small pieces and put on the bird table (robins can use them then as well) or in the scrap basket. Dripping, butchers trimmings and the like are all grist to the mill. Try pouring melted fat on the rough bark of branches or tree stumps and even allow yourself to throw it on the leaf litter, under hedges or brush wood where the wrens and dunnocks may pick up the scattered droplets when they congeal. The usual principle applies, that the more you can spread the food supply around the larger will be the number of beneficiaries and the more likely it is that the timid species will get their fair ration. One excellent way of making fats available is by the special bird cake outlined overleaf.

Coal tits and blue tits are expert at opening peanut shells.

*Individual aggression maintains a strict hierarchy among
the greenfinches visiting feeding tables.*

Special recipes

To make a basic 'bird cake' melt down any available fat you have – dripping, contents from the roast pan, bacon fat etc. Pour it into a basin and add any kitchen scraps, bird seed, peanuts, sultanas or other choice items you wish and allow the mix to cool and solidify. Turn it out of the basin (dip the basin in hot water if necessary) and then either hang the bird cake or put it on the bird table. You should make it in the approximate ratio of two parts food items to one part fat.

A more interesting way of presenting this cake is by making it directly into a half coconut shell (remember to fix a hanging string first!) or tit bell, or even in an empty yoghurt carton. You can place a piece of stick in the mix before it hardens to act as a learner's perch.

Edwin Cohen's pudding
80 oz (200 g) beef suet, 120 oz (300 g) coarse oatmeal, 2–3 oz (50–75 g) flour, 5 oz (125 g) water.
Mix flour and oatmeal with liquid fat and water to a stiff paste. Bake in a shallow pie dish to form a flat cake at 175°C (370°F) for approximately one hour.

Miss Turner's Maize Cake
Mix 3 oz (75 g) maize in a bowl with equal quantities of chopped nuts, hemp, canary and millet seed. Stir with boiling water until coagulated and add two beaten eggs. Tie tightly in a cloth and bake at 175°C (370°F) for 50 minutes–1 hour.

Tim's Bird Cake
2 lb (1 kg) self-raising flour, 8 oz (200 g) margarine, a little sugar.
Mix with water and bake like a rock bun.

Anti-sparrow pudding
Boil a cup of sugar with a cup of water for five minutes. Mix with a cup of melted fat and leave it to cool. Then mix with breadcrumbs, flour, birdseed, a little boiled rice and scraps until you have a very stiff mixture. Pack into any kind of can or jar. Lay the can on its side in a tree, on the window sill or any other place where birds can perch and pick out the food. Make sure the can is firm so that the birds will not dislodge it and rain does not get inside. It probably won't fool the sparrows for long, so don't take it too seriously.

Seeds

Finches and buntings are the principal seed-eaters among our garden birds, but whereas chaffinch and greenfinch will readily come to the bird table, other finches are much rarer – with the exception of siskin which increasingly comes to peanut feeders – and neither reed bunting nor yellowhammer are regular visitors to most gardens. In some years when weather is particularly hard or the beech mast crop is poor bramblings are regular visitors for seed supplies. Part of the successful role which chaffinch and greenfinch have achieved for themselves in the garden is due to the fact that both species are catholic seed eaters and will gladly take whatever is offered, the greenfinch in particular.

The only really efficient way to provide seed is from a hopper, usually the sort that can be fixed to the roof of the bird table as on the RSPB model, although the RSPB also markets a 13 in (32.5 cm) clearview columnar model with four feeding points at the base. However, a seed hopper does limit the range of birds which have access to the seed as all the seed-eating species are ground feeders. There is a case therefore for broadcasting some seed on the lawn to make it easier for yellowhammer, brambling, redpoll or siskin; but make sure the grass is very short or unfound seed may give you surprises the next year.

Bird seed mixes are widely available from pet shops and commercial wholesale suppliers. The mixes are variable in their content and you are advised to stick to a brand you know is reliable or go to the larger and most reputable suppliers. CJ Haith Ltd, Park Street, Cleethorpes have a good range of selections and EW Coombs Ltd, 25 Frindsbury Road, Strood, Kent are also reliable.

The biggest impact in this market for many years has been made by a new firm CJ Wildbird Foods Ltd of Upton Magna near Shrewsbury. They market peanuts, also a new high quality wildbird seed mix, and are the only firm currently marketing the irresistible peanut germ (which they advertise as 'peanut granules'). All the products are offered at highly competitive rates and a fast service.

Wherever you get the supply try to find out what the composition is before you buy. There should be plenty of canary grass in it and hemp, sunflower, niger, brassicas (rape etc) and millet — red or white.

Of the large grain seeds, wheat and barley are much used commercially for pheasant and partridge rearing and may well lure either species if you live in a country area where they are common. Greenfinches too love wheat and if you spread it on the ground well out in the open you may well find others coming too — collared dove, tree sparrow, feral pigeons and even the odd moorhen foraging from a nearby pond.

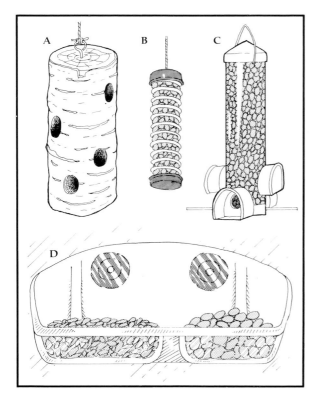

Different feeding devices.

KEY
A Suet stick
B Spiral peanut feeder
C Hanging seed feeder
D Double window feeder

Fruit

All the thrushes require a diet of fruit through the winter and when the weather gets hard, windfall apples from the autumn are the salvation of many redwings and fieldfares as well as our resident blackbirds, mistle and song thrushes. Keep all your unwanted apples in boxes in the shed until the weather is hard. Ask your greengrocer too if he can let you have spoiled or rotting ones. Spread the apples sparingly on the quieter areas of the garden when the weather is cold, but keep supplies back as long as possible for fear of running out when the need becomes greatest. From the turn of the New Year things will get difficult for them: the hawthorns and other berry-bearing bushes will have been stripped bare and if the weather is cold and the ground hard these thrushes will soon have a precarious time. Once the thrushes really need your apples they will arrive in big numbers. If apples are not available,

try pears or other soft fruit depending on what you can lay hands on.

Birds tend to waste an awful lot of berry fruits in the easy days of autumn, feeding when a high percentage of hawthorn, cotoneaster and others are spilled uneaten onto the ground to provide a feast for small mammals. It is a good idea to harvest some of this berry crop before the birds get to it and keep it for their time of greater need in winter. Either keep it in the deep freeze if space permits or air dry it and keep it in boxes in a safe cool store. Supply it later in the winter in small doses on the bird table or in one of the dispensers.

Many garden birds love dried fruit such as raisins, currants, sultanas or prunes and although you are unlikely to be much impressed with the idea of running supplies of such relatively expensive foods, you may decide to put some out when the need arises. Blackcaps have a soft spot for them which is worth bearing in mind, but soak the dried fruit overnight before putting it out.

Brambling occasionally visit garden feeders. Usually these winter visitors feed on fallen beech mast in woodlands.

Redwings and fieldfares feeding on fallen fruit in winter.

Meat

Meat scraps will be welcomed by some of the regular garden birds and are also likely to attract less frequent visitors — carrion crow, magpie, jackdaw — which you may or may not choose to encourage. Meat left around is a sure temptation for cats and dogs, and at night for rats and foxes so our advice is to use it sparingly. Tie a good marrow bone in a tree or suspend it from a bracket and the tits and nuthatch will thank you for it. Do not use uncooked meats, but limit the bird table supplies to scraps and trimmings cut off your joint.

Remember that tinned cat meat or dog meat is popular with many birds so use it if you need to. Also supplies of minced meat pass as very welcome worm and grub substitutes.

Live foods

Mealworms are the live food for birds second to none. Their supply and culture was discussed earlier (page 117). When they are supplied on the bird table they should be served up in a dish with sides which are sufficient to prevent escape before the birds have found them. Gentles are an acceptable alternative, as mentioned before, but are less pleasant to handle. 'Ant's eggs' as supplied by angling shops are another relished morsel. They are actually the ant pupae rather than eggs and you can collect these yourself if you want to seek them out from the colonies under logs or flagstones; put the logs and flags back again afterwards so that the damage can be made good and the colony not left open to predators all and sundry.

Foods to avoid

Dessicated coconut should never be used as it will swell up inside the birds and may kill them. Avoid highly spiced foods and curry remains, most cooked fruits and vegetables and the slushy remains of meals. Remember that poultry bones put out to let the birds clean them off, can be lethal to cats and dogs because they splinter so easily. Taken in excessive quantity, salt is toxic to birds, affecting the nervous system, so ensure that large amounts do not find their way onto the bird table food. The amounts that normally occur in smoked bacon rinds or salted peanuts (but wash the peanuts as described on page 126) are unlikely to be harmful. However, do not feed potato crisps.

To feed a wren

Wrens are one of most people's favourite garden birds, but because they are fairly strictly insectivorous all the year round they are very difficult to attract to the feeding station and therefore very difficult to help in times of hardship. One or two ways have been suggested where tempting morsels might succeed when they are put in the right place. Wrens are great troglodytes and explorers of the dark and shady hedge bottoms and ivy-covered walls. Select a place where you know they regularly forage, or even build a brushwood bundle yourself in a suitable corner, and try scattering finely grated cheese, minced meat or tiny fragments of dog meat in such places. Keep an eye on it and see if the wrens mop it up; if so try rewarding them with a modest supply of 'ant-eggs' — they will like them best of all.

Urban jackdaws love to play in the smoke plumes from chimneys on house tops.

Feeding devices

A variety of feeding devices has already been described but the field is a wide and expanding one and there is plenty of choice. It is not possible to mention more than a small selection of the best of those which can be employed and these are illustrated and described on the following pages. Bear in mind the warnings about cheap, sharp and dangerous designs and stick to the reliable and proven suppliers when you are purchasing items.

The following suppliers can be relied upon and will send you a full catalogue on request.

RSPB, The Lodge, Sandy, Bedfordshire
SG19 2DL

Scandinavian Designs, 13 Hillside Road,
Marlow, Bucks SL17 3JU

Scottish National Institute for the War Blinded,
Linburn, Wilkieston, by Kirknewton,
Midlothian.

Smoke bathing

Jackdaws are well adapted to urban and suburban living and, although fairly shy and cautious, will make rapid excursions to a bird table to snatch large items and fly off with them. In the season of course they may well try to nest in the house chimney. In late summer and autumn they have another, even stranger, association with chimneys. In an activity that is probably partly heat bathing and partly yet another function of feather maintenance jackdaws will sit on the chimney tops where either hot air or smoke is rising and open and shake their wings as the hot fumes engulf them. Or if the chimney is large and the emission strong they may drift round and round in the rising column until it supports them no more and they will drop down to start again.

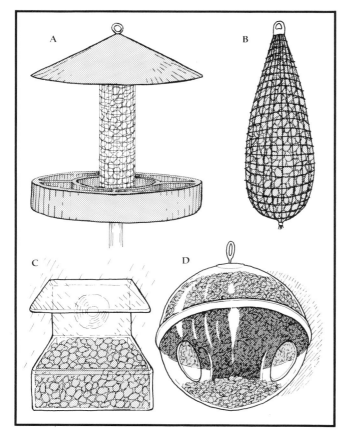

Bird feeding devices.

KEY
A Bird house feeder
B Bag of nuts
C RSPB shelter feeder
D Space feeder

Putty pecking paper strippers

In some autumns blue tits and great tits will suddenly switch from being mild and inoffensive
garden dwellers to out and out domestic vandals.
Paper stripping is the name of the game and at
such times the tits will shred newspapers or maga-
zines, strip pieces of wallpaper and even attack
paper lampshades, putting the house under siege
on occasions to the extent of requiring windows
and doors to be kept closed for a few days. These
irregular bouts of paper tearing have long been
recognised – as far back as 1949 the British Trust
for Ornithology carried out a national enquiry
into the subject – and at times the tits determined
autumn assaults on houses in their frenzied efforts
to explore are more amusing than annoying. The
purpose of this strange habit is a little confused. It
is certainly not related to shortage of food, as
often birds will leave a loaded bird table to renew
an assault on nearby windows in an attempt to
break and enter. It is prevalent on dry, warm
autumn days (it often stops when a wet spell sets
in) and appears to be most likely in seasons when
populations are particularly high. The shredding
of paper, and particularly the stripping of wallpaper, have much in common with the stripping
and exploring of bark in the quest for insects, and
although no comprehensive explanation exists it
seems likely to be a combination of the compelling
urge to hunt (whether or not good food supplies
abound), a need to explore, and a reaction to the
stress of high numbers.

Putty pecking is a similar phenomenon but this
may involve not only tits but magpies or starlings
– even partridges and carrion crows have been
claimed to indulge! When the habit is persistently
repeated on newly puttied windows it can become
annoying. The birds sometimes seem to become
addicted to the fishy taste of the linseed oil
although it is doubtful that they actually eat much,
if any, of it. It is a habit which has become more
prevalent in recent years, perhaps as more tits and
other birds are forced into suburban cohabitation
with man. To stop the habit, try mixing pepper or
paraffin with the putty when you replace it or tack
panel pins into the putty and thread black cotton
between them; beware it is not done in such a way
that the birds can become entangled. As an alternative if the problem remains serious, try a hard
polyurethane paint, or fabric sealing strips, to
cover the putty.

Both of these habits particularly involve young
birds – so we can blame it on juvenile delinquency
once again. The explanation we particularly like is
one put forward seriously some years ago; that in
dry autumn weather the tits readily become
intoxicated by a surplus of alcohol-rich elderberries with the result that such behaviour can be
attributed to simple drunken disorderliness!

DECEMBER

Pecking for power

On a busy day the milling crowd at the bird table is in an endless round of disputes, threats and squabbles. They may all appear random and bad tempered, but like other aspects of a bird's daily life there is a structure and purpose to it all. Obviously the largest and more aggressive species are dominant over others when there is competition and communal feeding; starlings will cause robins, tits and finches to scatter, great tits and blue tits will step aside for a nuthatch on the nut feeder and the nuthatch in its turn will give way to a great spotted woodpecker.

As well as this ordering between the different species there is often also a well developed ranking within each species. It is most advanced in the flocking birds. Every schoolboy knows that a firm pecking order is employed by domestic chickens, but the same ranking also applies within wild bird families too. The 'top bird' amongst the great tits at the feeder is probably an old male who has slowly won his way to the pole position through the long term investment of a pugnacious nature and stepping into dead men's shoes. Greenfinches are the commonest of the bird table feeders which show this hierarchy of dominance very clearly. Again it is usually a big and well coloured male who is dominant and he will resist the competition of others, and all will step away to follow him to feed. Below him the peck order is equally well structured; the number two is dominant over all others except the top bird; the number three moves aside only for numbers one and two . . . and so on and so on.

Although a peck order may seem hard on those at the bottom – usually this year's youngsters – it actually has advantages for all. The benefit to the dominant birds is obvious: they have first claim on food whenever they need it. The recognition of their senior rank by others removes the need for constant battles and the wasted energy they involve for both senior and junior members. The advantage to the subordinates is equally strong in that they know their place and recognise that they must wait their turn or save time and move to an alternative place to search. They still gain from being part of the flock however, instead of living an individual life outside it, because they benefit from the fact that a large flock of birds is much more likely to find the really good feeding places than an individual bird on its own. The law of survival-of-the-fittest applies in times of hard weather and food shortage. Then it is the dominant birds – the strongest, best and fittest – who will survive to breed in the following summer. Death will climb upwards on a straight ladder through the pecking order.

A bird for Christmas

Almost every Christmas card reminds us that the robin is far more the Christmas bird, even than the unfortunate turkey. Although it has become an indispensable part of the legend of Christmas the robin's association with the feast does not date back very far in time. The origins derive from the fact that Victorian postmen wore bright red frock coats and were, not surprisingly, nicknamed 'robins'; thus the association of robins with Christmas cards and thence Christmas itself.

The poor wren has much less auspicious connections, epitomised in the curious and ancient custom of the 'wren hunt'. The tradition has various suggested origins but a popular Christmas one is that the wren prevented St Stephen escaping by hopping onto the gaoler's shoulder and awaking him at the crucial moment, a deed for which the tiny troglodyte has paid for dearly ever since. Throughout the centuries the 'wren hunt' was performed in various forms in different parts of Britain and some areas of mainland Europe. The date for the wren hunt was not constant in all areas but traditionally occurred on St Stephen's Day, 26th December (now less interestingly called Boxing Day). In a singularly unfriendly and primitive activity the wretched wren was hunted down through lanes and hedgerows and, when eventually caught, was ritually killed. Its minute corpse was then borne in ceremony through town or village on an elaborate bier or 'wren house', carried by grotesquely dressed 'wren boys' to the accompaniment of pipes, flutes, drums or whistle while coins were solicited 'for the burial'. The tradition was very widely practiced well into the present century from places as far apart as County Kerry to Suffolk and the Isle of Man to the south coast. In Wales the ultimate pardox was chanted as they carried the wretched corpse, 'Cussed is the man who kills robin or wren'!

The robin, nowadays revered as our national bird, has not always escaped a similar fate to that of the wren. Despite the fact (as legend has us believe) that the robin scorched its breast in collecting fire from Hell for the benefit of man on earth, our thanks to our small friend were somewhat short lived and we are told of the great virtues of fresh robin roasted on the spit. Beware however, for if you should happen to use a hazel

The robin is our most popular bird although this has not always protected it from harsh treatment in the past.

stick for the spit the robin — we are assured — will rotate itself and roast unaided. Don't bother to try it; stick with the Christmas turkey — it's bigger and juicier and you can always put the carcass on the bird table for the robin to peck at.

BTO Garden Bird Survey

In the winter of 1970/71 the British Trust for Ornithology launched the Garden Bird Feeding Survey with the main aims of determining which species make use of gardens at different times of year; what range of foods is provided in gardens and which are the preferred ones. Since then bird gardeners and other householders — sometimes with little more than a backyard and a window box — have contributed to the survey from all parts of the country. In the first ten years of the survey alone, 199 different species were recorded in gardens for which observations were sent in!

The mind boggles at the gardens which produced wigeon, red kite, Bewick's swan and an American blue jay. What is proved beyond dispute by the survey is the enormous range of species which do, from one time to another, make use of our gardens and the important part which all these gardens play for birds in our ever-shrinking countryside.

Another important fact disclosed is the extent to which the number and variety of birds differs from year to year depending on the severity of the winter. The conclusion is clear: garden bird feeding in winter is a major contributor to the survival of many of our individual birds.

Seventeen years on from the start of the Survey the BTO has now revamped and expanded it, generously sponsored by the electronics firm BASF. Launched in autumn 1987 the survey seeks to attract up to 5,000 participating garden enthusiasts all of whom are supplied with special recording forms and are asked to record details of the use

*The various common species of tits are first to make use of
food supplies provided in the garden.*

which different birds make of the garden – not just the feeding station, as in earlier years – right through the year. So, if *you* want to become one of Britain's official, garden bird recorders write to the BTO, Beech Grove, Tring, Herts and they would be pleased to hear from you, whether you have a two-acre spread in Sunningdale, a backyard in Halifax or a lighthouse compound in the Irish Sea.

The 'new' Garden Bird Survey not only produces a lot more detail about birds' feeding preferences in gardens but also provides important information on the extent to which different breeding species use our gardens for nesting in different parts of the country. Special emphasis too is placed on one or two species which are currently declining on farmland and which make some use of gardens, for example linnet and tree sparrow, and magpies which have increased rapidly in suburban gardens in recent years and are accused of undue depletion of garden song birds.

One question which the bird gardener wants answered most is 'What are the top garden species?' The seventeen years of the survey so far undertaken can give this answer with authority.

Although the relative position of each of the commonest species may vary a little from one year to the next, the Top Twelve are usually as follows (based on the percentage of gardens in which they are recorded).

Blue tit	Great tit
Blackbird	Greenfinch
Robin	Starling
House sparrow	Song thrush
Dunnock	Coal tit
Chaffinch	Collared dove

In most years these twelve are followed, a few percentage points behind, by wren, magpie, mistle thrush, black-headed gull and pied wagtail. Not surprisingly, with all this bounty of feathered food on hand, the sparrowhawk comes around twentieth place. Whether or not you take part in the BTO's Garden Bird Survey, keep a list of all the species you see in your garden; it will surprise you and encourage you to go on trying to add to the list.

The BTO's Garden Bird Survey confirms robin and blackbird as two of our commonest garden birds.

Binoculars

A good pair of binoculars is virtually indispensible, even for the birdwatcher limited to his garden. The problem is that the range of binoculars is enormous and the choice quickly becomes bewildering. Assuming that one is talking about a first pair of binoculars you should aim to find a pair which suits your purse, is reasonably light in weight and gives a bright image over a medium field of view. Binocular specifications are given by two figures, eg 8 × 35; '8' indicates the size of magnification and '35' tells you that the diameter of the object lens (the big end of the binoculars!) is 35 mm across. You should select a pair which is eight, nine or ten magnification, with an object lens between thirty and fifty millimeters. Ideal combinations for general use and certainly applicable to garden birdwatching are 8 × 30, 8 × 40 or 10 × 40. Whatever happens, do not select a magnification greater than 10 because you will be unable to hold them steady in your hands without producing a wobbly image. Take the opportunity of looking through other people's glasses to find out what suits you best. Avoid zoom binoculars, which will be heavy and unnecessarily expensive, and any pairs which have blurring around the edges of the image or show colour halo effects.

Once you have determined the power and size which suits you the best advice is to buy the most expensive you can afford, although at these first stages it may be prudent to stay nearer the bottom end of the market. The relatively cheap 'Avocet' binoculars marketed by the RSPB are a good buy. Write for a catalogue and price list, (address on page 141).

Nowadays the sparrowhawk is a successful urban and suburban hunter as well as being primarily a rural bird.

ADDRESSES OF SUPPLIERS MENTIONED IN THE BOOK

CJ Wildbird Foods Ltd, The Rea, Upton Magna, nr Shrewsbury, SY4 4UB
Range of first class bird foods.

Henry Doubleday Research Association, National Centre for Organic Gardening, Ryton-on-Dunsmore, Coventry CV8 3LG
Organic gardening advice and supplies; safe pesticides, crop protection, wildflower seeds, cultivated attrodant plants.

RSPB, The Lodge, Sandy, Bedfordshire SG19 2DL
The widest selection of high quality garden bird furniture, nest boxes, feeding devices, bird tables, binoculars, clothing etc.

Pippaware, 122 Ennerdale Road, Richmond-on-Thames TW9 2DH
Wild bird feeding table and 'Happy Bird' nest box.

Jamie Wood Ltd, Cross Street, Polegate, Sussex
Bird furniture, hides, nest boxes (including tawny owl, little owl and woodpecker), feeding devices including Sussex bird table.

Scottish National Institution for the War Blinded, Linburn, Wilkieston, by Kirknewton, Midlothian
Feeding devices, nest boxes, bird tables.

Nerine Nurseries, Welland, Malvern, Worcs. WR13 6LN
Bird tables, nest boxes, feeding devices and best artificial house martin nests.

National Trust Shop, Killerton, Broadclyst, Devon EX5 3LE
Glazed pottery bird bell in smart box.

Septico (Slug Killer), 184 Henwood Road, Tettenhall, Wolverhampton, W. Midlands

---

BIBLIOGRAPHY

Bromhall, D *Devil Birds*, Hutchinson 1980
du Feu, C *Nest Boxes* (BTO Guide 20), BTO 1985
Everett, MJ *Garden Birds*, The Apple Press 1985
Feare, C *The Starling*, OUP 1984
Glue, D *The Garden Bird Book*, MacMillan 1982
Lack, D *The Life of the Robin*, Pelican 1943
Lack, P *Atlas of Wintering Birds in Britain and Ireland*, BTO and IWC 1986
Newton, I *Finches*, Collins 1972
Perrins, CM *British Tits*, Collins 1979

RSPB, *Gardening with Wildlife* 1982
RSPB, Various information and advisory leaflets
Sharrock, T *Atlas of Breeding Birds in Britain and Ireland*, BTO and IWC 1976
Simms, E *Thrushes*, Collins 1978
Simms, E *Warblers*, Collins 1985
Soper, T *The Bird Table Book*, David & Charles 1986
Soper, T *Discovering Birds*, BBC 1983
Wood, N *Birds in your Garden*, Hamlyn 1985

Blue tit

Coal tit

Great tit

Male house sparrow

Female house sparrow

Tree sparrow

Female chaffinch

Male chaffinch

Marsh tit

Willow tit

Garden warbler

Male linnet

Male greenfinch

Female blackcap

Male blackcap

Willow warbler

Goldfinch

Nuthatch

Male siskin

Song thrush

Juvenile blackbird

Male redpoll

Spotted flycatcher

Mistle thrush

Collared dove

Sparrowhawk

ACKNOWLEDGEMENTS

The authors wish to acknowledge the help of the many individual garden birdwatchers who gave advice and commented on a host of items in this book. We thank also David Glue (BTO) and various staff of the RSPB for their contributions.

Margaret Anthony, who typed the text, deserves our special thanks.